The LT Area

1: South East London

Visions International Entertainment Ltd

Much of outer South East London is hilly, and one of its most spectacular steep hills is the aptly-named Corkscrew Hill in West Wickham. On 1st September 1972, RT225 (TB) has just passed one of its fellows working route 119 between Bromley North and West Croydon at one of its many twists and turns. In snowy weather, passengers often had to alight from their buses to help them struggle up this steep hill and even in some cases help push them!

The LT Area

1: South East London

Published by Visions International Entertainment Limited

ISBN: 978-1-9126952-7-0

Visions International Entertainment Limited
The Billiard Room, Parklands Farm, Lower Green, Chelmsford, Essex, CM2 8QS
e-mail: deltic15@aol.com

For details of other bus and transport-related products, please visit the Visions web site:
http://www.visionsinternational.biz

Contents

Introduction

This book is the first in a new series looking at London Transport bus operations covering various parts of the former L.T. Central Area. We begin in South East London. Once again I have combed my extensive archives to provide fresh material, since the vast majority of the 360 or so photographs included herein have not been published before. Most of the pictures were taken between 1967, at the dawn of the disastrous "Reshaping" era, and 1984, when London Transport was destroyed by the Thatcher regime. However, there are also some more recent scenes, to give a flavour of how the area covered has changed subsequently.

By "South East London", I mean those areas with London SE postcodes, together with those parts of West Kent incorporated into Greater London in 1965 and served anyway by red Central Area buses. I have basically taken the A23 Brighton Road as the dividing line between "South East" and "South West" London, though am including most of the Croydon area routes, including those serving New Addington, in the "South West" volume. I am not including Country Area/London Country and Green Line services which intruded into the former Central Area in these new volumes, having dealt with these adequately in the recent "Roadside" volume specifically featuring them, and my earlier book "Country Cousins".

A quick browse through this new volume will immediately reveal the considerable number of RT-types featured. This is only coincidentally because, in their last ten years or so, I concentrated very heavily on them.

The main reason so many RT-types appear in these pages is simply that there were so many of them working in South East London, right up to their final full year of operation, 1978. In turn, there are two reasons for this. One is that many routes working in the area were (and some still are!) tram replacement routes.

Owing to the interruption by World War Two of London Transport's 1935-1940 New Works Programme, under which the vast majority of trams were to have been replaced by trolleybuses, all trams based in the area survived the war, except for those working from Bexleyheath and Carshalton depots, at which trolleybuses had been introduced early on. These trams had been left until the last to convert to trolleybuses, since the majority were former London County Council trams, which mostly worked from the third centre-rail conduit system of electrification rather than from overhead wires. It was obviously easier to convert tram routes using the latter system, the majority of which were in West, North and East London, to trolleybus operation first.

After the war, it was decided to convert all surviving tram routes to motor bus operation instead, and RT-types were used to replace trams at such depots as Abbey Wood, New Cross, Walworth (formerly named Camberwell) and also new bus garages built for tram replacement routes such as Peckham and Rye Lane in the area covered by this book. And less than seven years after the last trams

had gone, the two isolated trolleybus systems serving the area were replaced by RTs, too.

Another reason why so many RTs were based in the area was that very few other types were. As at 1967, for example, only three routes, the 202 and associated 202A and the 227, needed single-deckers (RFs) owing to low bridges, and no RLHs at all were based in the area. Moreover, RMs came very late to the area, since aside from a very small allocation at Elmers End Garage introduced in 1960 in association with the replacement of trolleybus route 630, which ran all the way from Willesden Junction to West Croydon, they were not based in South East London until November 1961, when trolleybus replacement route 141 was extended from Moorgate all the way down to Grove Park, replacing RTs on route 179 (which itself was a tram replacement service) and introducing new RMs to New Cross Garage. And it was not until early 1963, when Rye Lane and then Peckham Garages received them for routes 36A and 36B (RL) and 36 (PM) which, with the 63 following at the latter garage in the autumn of that year, that new RMs were allocated to the area for traditional trunk routes.

Between 1964 and 1968, such trunk routes as the 35, 40, 45, 53 and 171 received secondhand examples, but it was not until the autumn of the latter year that any suburban route in outer South East London received them, and this was the 180. Many major trunk routes serving the area retained RTs well into the 1970s: the long and winding route 12 did not receive them until early 1973, and the 1, 21 and 47 until two years later. Most outer-suburban routes using RMs did not get them until as late as 1976/77, for example the 51/A, 161/A, 228 and 229 - all replacing the faithful RTs, and indeed Bromley and Catford Garages were jointly the penultimate garages to operate RTs in the entire fleet, when they were replaced by RMs on route 94 at the end of August 1978, finally bringing to an end RT-type operation in the area after some thirty years. It was not for nothing that the areas around Bexley, Eltham, Sidcup and Woolwich were referred to as "RT Land" fifty-odd years ago, since no other types of bus were based there! In contrast, RM-operation on outer suburban routes in the area was very short-lived indeed, all had been replaced by O.P.O. types by mid-1986.

Although I have always lived in North London, I soon got to know London's buses routes "over the water" very well too, thanks to my frequent visits there - as the photographs in this new book will show. In closing, may I put on record my thanks, as usual, to Colin Clarke who scanned my vast collection of negatives to make these volumes possible and also, Michael J. McClelland for laying out the book and of course, to my publisher Ken Carr for doing such a good job producing them!

Jim Blake
1st February 2020

Main Cover Photo: For many years, RT-types dominated South East London, so much so enthusiasts dubbed it "RT Land"! One of the main centres of their operation was Eltham, and on 28th May 1968, Saunders-bodied roofbox RT3924 (SP) crosses the junction of Eltham High Street and Well Hall Road on busy trunk route 21 bound for Moorgate, with three other RTs for company.

Top Left Cover Photo: In common with most other parts of London, South East London had to suffer the awful DMSs during the 1970s and early 1980s. On 27th October 1982, a packed B20 DMS2383 (BX) approaches Woolwich town centre on route 122A. Soon, these would be replaced by new Titans and concentrated in South West London's Wandle District, although ironically, earlier DMSs which were actually repurchased from Scottish operators worked at Bexleyheath Garage under the cheapskate "Bexleybus" remit for a couple of years at the end of the 1980s.

Top Right Cover Photo: On New Year's Day 1983, brand new Titan T569 (PD) changes crew opposite Plumstead Garage working local route 178. These were rapidly replacing the last remaining MDs at the time, as well as ousting surviving DMSs in South East London, which they came to dominate in the later 1980s and early 1990s.

Back Cover Photo: Typifying the buses that dominated South East London for best part of thirty years, RT1881 (AM) has unusually terminated at Woolwich Arsenal Station, and its conductor has put its passengers off: "there's another one behind!". The date is Saturday 15th April 1978 and a notice on the bus stop warns of the changes that will take place in the area a week later, when the RTs' domination will finally end - leaving just those working route 94 to soldier on for another four months.

Down By The Thames

Several routes in South East London ran close to the southern bank of the River Thames. The river is not far away as RT3114 (SP) calls at Surrey Docks Station on 21st September 1968. Behind it are the warehouses of the then still busy Surrey Commercial Docks. This RT was one of several "GB Plate" buses, which had travelled overseas promoting London and usually retained not only their GB plates, but also their original bodies at overhaul. Route 228 was withdrawn north of Eltham, Well Hall Station five weeks after this picture was taken, replaced by a diversion of route 108A.

Erith is one of the closest points where buses come to the river in outer South East London, and on 15th April 1970, RT4064 (BX) heads along its High Street. Of note is the trolleybus traction standard still in use to support a road sign, whereas it has been rendered redundant otherwise both by a new bus stop, and a new street lighting column! Trolleybuses had been replaced here more than eleven years previously in the first stage of the conversion programme, in which route 132 had been extended to Erith to supplement the 229 (which replaced trolleybus 698), and subsequently to Woolwich. Three days after this picture was taken, the route converted to SM O.M.O. and was diverted/truncated to terminate at Slade Green Station instead.

Route 168A, which originally ran from Turnpike Lane to Clapham Junction, skirted part of South East London by running alongside the Thames on Albert Embankment. On a snowy 31st January 1972, RT2104 (HT) heads along there, calling outside Queensborough House which was then an "outstation" of County Hall at which I was employed. The large building on the left is the London Fire Brigade Headquarters. This route converted to crew DM three years later and has subsequently disappeared.

Still in existence today, route 185 is one of many tram replacement routes in South East London, originally running from Victoria to Lewisham via Camberwell, with rush hour extensions to Delta Metal Works, literally above the Blackwall Tunnel. On 14th April 1973, RT4285 (TL) works one of these journeys, passing the southern entrance to the original, now northbound, Blackwall Tunnel. The route converted to DMS O.M.O. four weeks later. Today, the industrial area this route served is long gone, with such structures as the Millennium Dome dominating the area.

With quite a wide expanse of the Thames in the background, a shabby RT1957 (BX) speeds up the hill out of Erith bound for Orpington on the 229. Nine days later, this route was withdrawn west of Erith (replaced between there and Woolwich by new O.P.O. DMS route 269) and converted to RM operation.

Next day, on 13th May 1977, RT2758 (AW) disgorges shoppers in Woolwich Church Street when working the 161A's rush hour extension to Charlton Station. Woolwich Dockyard is on the left. This route also converted to RM operation on 21st May 1977, later being in effect merged with the parent 161.

Dockside buildings are visible on the left, along with the appropriately-named Watermans Arms on the right, as RM599 (TL) turns short at Charlton Station on 14th September 1978. At the time worked jointly between Abbey Wood and Catford Garages, tram replacement route 180 was the first outer suburban route in South East London to gain a full allocation of RMs, just under ten years before this picture was taken.

Not far from where the previous picture was taken, DMS178 (NX) runs home along Woolwich Road to New Cross Garage in the evening rush hour of 13th October 1981. The 177 was another tram replacement route, which received these awful vehicles in replacement of RTs in January 1972. Two years after this picture was taken, Titans replaced them on New Cross' share of the 177. They had already replaced the MDs which had briefly worked it from Abbey Wood and then the new Plumstead Garage.

By 4th September 1982, when savage cuts to services hastened by the Thatcher regime not only caused the first withdrawals of standard RMs but also decimated the ranks of non-B20 DMSs, DMS1905 (NX) was in a rapidly diminishing minority! It departs from Greenwich Seamens' hospital, beside the Thames, on route 188 bound for Euston. This was yet another tram replacement route, whose RTs were replaced by SMSs in March 1971, which in turn succumbed to DMSs.

Not far from the same spot on 28th June 1986, another New Cross bus, RM1048 (NX) has arrived on a Sunday working of route 1. The famous Cutty Sark in its dry dock forms an impressive backdrop. Hitherto, the number 1A had been used for Sunday workings here. A year later, the 1 converted to Titan O.P.O.

Roundabouts

A number of roundabouts feature on bus routes serving South East London, one of the first of which encountered on crossing the Thames is that at the southern end of Waterloo Bridge. Built in the early 1960s and comprising an unattractive all-concrete bowl connecting with predestrian subways, it soon became a haunt of drug dealers and prostitutes, then latterly the homeless. In recent times, a large cinema has been built there. On 15th January 1968, Saunders-bodied RT3107 (WL) rounds it on the 171's long journey from Tottenham to Forest Hill. This was one of three routes that replaced the Kingsway Subway trams, and at the time this picture was taken my route to "work" at nearby County Hall from Canonbury. RMs took over upon "Reshaping" on 7th September 1968, with the Walworth share being transferred to New Cross Garage.

Another well-known roundabout in South East London is that at Elephant & Castle, which, however, in line with recent trends is being removed as this book is being compiled. On 11th April 1968, RTL381 (AR) is followed around it by an RT on route 12. Tottenham was the 171's other garage at this time, and RTs briefly replaced the RTLs between 14th June and 6th September 1968. Today, the once lengthy 171 only runs only between here and Catford Garage via Forest Hill! In this picture, bomb damage from the heavy blitz of 10th May 1941 is still all too evident.

The second roundabout encountered on entering South East London is that at the southern end of Westminster Bridge. Again created out of bomb-damaged properties, it is nearing completion on 16th April 1969 as Saunders-bodied RT1204 (WL) heads around it for a clockwise trip around Victoria Embankment on tram replacement route 184. No sooner had its builder, the Greater London Council, landscaped and grassed the new roundabout than they ripped it all up again to build a new Island Block linked to their adjacent County Hall headquarters! This was much to the outrage of the Ministry of Transport, who had given them funding to build the thing for highway improvement - NOT to enlarge County Hall. I should know, as I "worked" in the relevant G.L.C. admin office at the time! Meanwhile, the 184 converted to DMS O.M.O. in October 1971.

The Bricklayers Arms junction was another G.L.C. road "improvement" scheme at this period, where both a roundabout and a flyover were put in at the junction of the Old and New Kent Roads and Tower Bridge Road. This time, a problem they had was encountering "unexpected" tracks and complicated pointwork for trams beneath the road surface! Odd that, considering their predecessor the London County Council had built them in the first place for their trams! Once again, I know of this from my "work" at County Hall. Works are in full swing as RT4448 (Q) heads north on the short 42 route on 3rd January 1970. This route converted to "recycled" ex-Red Arrow O.M.O. MB operation three weeks later.

Central Croydon suffered badly at the hands of the Luftwaffe during the Blitz, not least owing to the proximity of Croydon Aerodrome. During the 1950s and early 1960s, much of the town centre was redeveloped as a result, not least the junction of Wellesley Road and George Street, where both a roundabout and an underpass were built. On 27th May 1970, RT344 (ED) passes the junction on route 194, which converted to SMS O.M.O. five months later. Croydon's trams cross this junction today.

A roundabout at the southern end of Orpington High Street houses a war memorial. On 1st September 1972, RT1547 (SP) passes it on route 51A bound for Green Street Green. This route would have a very short-lived RM allocation for a few weeks in early 1977, before being effectively renumbered 51 and converted to DMS O.P.O. in May.

On 3rd October 1972, RT4283 (A) negotiates the roundabout at the top of Anerley Hill, to stand at the Crystal Palace terminus of route 154. Converted from trolleybus route 654 in the first stage of the conversion programme in March 1959, this route succumbed to DMS O.M.O. in May 1973.

With a background of monstrous 1960s buildings erected to replace those damaged in the Blitz, RT1066 (NX) rounds the Elephant & Castle roundabout on 21st February 1975, the last day of full RT operation from New Cross Garage on route 1. This was progressively converted to RM operation from Catford Garage over the previous four weeks, and then similarly dealt with at New Cross. However, RTs continued to substitute for RMs right up until the end of RT operation in South East London in August 1978.

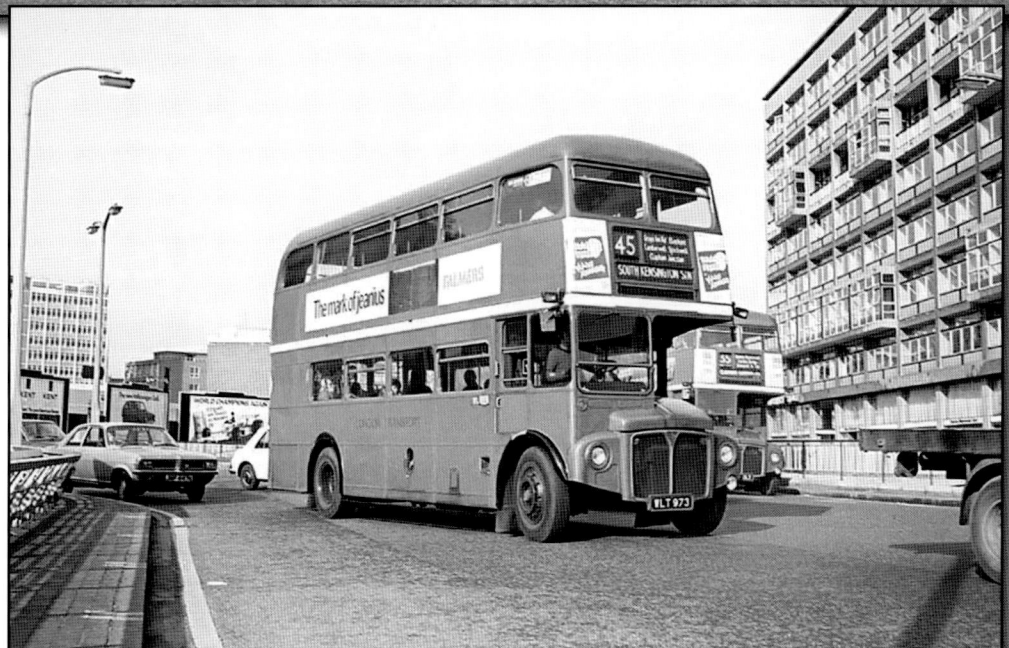

Heading in the opposite direction on the same occasion is RM973 (WL) on the very circuitous route 45, which trundled all the way through Walworth, Camberwell, Brixton, Stockwell, Clapham and Battersea to reach South Kensington. Two days after this picture was taken, the route converted to crew DM, thus providing RMs to replace route 1's RTs. RMs returned in the spring of 1981, remaining until the route's O.P.O. conversion in August 1985.

Route 21 was another to convert from RT to RM at this period, and on the final day of RT operation, RT1540 (SP) negotiates the Yorkshire Grey roundabout in Eltham, heading home to Sidcup Garage. RTs subbed for RMs on this route until the spring of 1977, when they were finally removed from Sidcup Garage.

Trolleybus replacement route 141 replaced the 641 between Winchmore Hill and Moorgate in November 1961, and then on weekdays was extended along London Wall to St. Paul's, from where it replaced route 179 all the way to Grove Park. At first, route 141A ran at weekends following the 179's route exactly from Grove Park to Finsbury Park until withdrawn nearly ten years later. On 12th March 1977, RM1681 (NX) turns off the Bricklayers Arms roundabout into the Old Kent Road and has been unusually curtailed at Catford Garage. A week later, this route also converted to crew DM operation, having to suffer them for some five years before RMs returned. It converted to O.P.O. early in 1985.

On the same day as the previous picture, RT2944 (SP) negotiates the roundabout at the junction of the Sidcup By-Pass and Sevenoaks Way at Foots Cray. Route 229 had originally been a single-deck route in this area, and featured in the first stage of the trolleybus conversion programme in March 1959 by being extended from Bexleyheath to Woolwich, replacing route 698. Two months after this picture was taken, it converted to RM operation and was withdrawn west of Erith, as well as being diverted at Orpington to replace the 51's section of route to Farnborough. O.P.O. conversion followed in September 1982 when it was cut back again to Orpington.

Routes 161 and 161A followed each other between Woolwich and Chislehurst, from where the 161 continued to Sidcup Garage, whilst the 161A continued to Petts Wood Station. Both routes also had rush hour extensions from Woolwich to Charlton Station. On 20th May 1977, the last day of RT operation on both routes, RT3997 (AW) circumnavigates the roundabout at the junction of Chislehurst Road and Petts Wood Road. The two routes were combined as the 161 in September 1980 and O.P.O. conversion followed in February 1985.

Negotiating one of the small "white spot" roundabouts in Blackheath Village, RT4619 (TL) is turning short at Elmers End Green rather than working the 54's full route from Woolwich to Croydon on 19th April 1978. The route converted to DMS O.P.O. three days later as part of "Bus Plan '78 Stage One".

On a garage journey of route 161A back to Abbey Wood Garage, RM270 (AW) passes Well Hall Road roundabout in Eltham on 11th September 1978. When that garage closed in October 1981, the allocation moved to the new Plumstead Garage from where crew MDs replaced RMs until supplanted by Titans, still initially crew-operated, early in 1983.

Trolleybus replacement route 149 skirted the inner edge of South East London between Blackfriars and Lambeth Bridges on its weekday extension beyond Liverpool Street to Victoria. On 2nd April 1981, former Green Line coach RCL2229 (SF) rounds the roundabout at the southern end of Lambeth Bridge during their brief tenure of the route. It is now preserved at the L.T. Museum.

Route 149 also circumnavigated the Addington Street roundabout at the southern end of Westminster Bridge, as RCL2246 (SF) does when unusually curtailed from the south to Dalston, Downham Road on 20th July 1981. This view shows how these former coaches had their rear platform doors removed for use as red buses, as well as the monstrous County Hall Island Block, illicitly erected by the Greater London Council in the middle of the roundabout. Disused for years after the G.L.C.'s abolition by the Thatcher Regime in 1986, it was demolished early in the present century and a plush hotel stands there now. Meanwhile, the 149 had reverted to RM operation by the end of 1984 and converted to O.P.O. early in 1987. Subsequently worked by bendibuses, its southern terminus today is London Bridge Station.

A second roundabout is located at the junction of Walworth Road and Newington Butts at the Elephant & Castle. On 22nd April 1982, RM990 (WL) heads for Cannon Street there on the rush hour 176A. This tram replacement route differed from the parent 176 by continuing from the Elephant via Borough and Southwark Bridge to Cannon Street Station, rather than to Waterloo and the West End, and was withdrawn amid the "Law Lords" service cuts of September 1982.

Terminus

The crew of RT189 (TB) changes over at route 138's Bromley North Station terminus on 9th December 1967. This short route converted to 50-seat conventional O.M.O. MBs in May 1969, later graduating to DMSs and then to Titans.

Also on the Bromley North Station terminus that day in North Street is crew-operated RF407 (TB), which has unusually been curtailed on the busy 227 at nearby Bromley Market Place. During the 1960s, this route was the only major RF-operated Central Area bus service in the whole of South East London, running from Crystal Palace to Chislehurst. It converted to SMS O.M.O. in early January 1971.

In the heart of "RT Land", Eltham Well Hall Southern Region Station was adjoined by a sizeable bus station, which catered not only for a variety of routes which terminated there, but also for short workings on such routes as the 21. It also had a London Transport canteen were crews took their breaks, beside which Saunders-bodied RT3088 (NX) stands on 27th December 1967 - my 20th birthday! Route 89 was a horseshoe-shaped service at this time, which ran from Eltham to Lewisham, via Bexley, Welling, Shooters Hill and Blackheath. It converted to DMS O.P.O. in April 1978. Unfortunately, both the railway and bus stations were swept away by an extension of the M2 motorway in the 1980s. A new Eltham railway station and bus terminus replaced them on the eastern side of Well Hall Road, also replacing nearby Eltham Park Station.

Several bus routes terminated in the forecourt of Peckham Garage, one of them being Peckham & Nunhead Circular route 173. On 9th March 1969, RM1232 (RL) lays over there working nearby Rye Lane Garage's weekend allocation on the route, a fortnight before that garage closed. On the right of the picture is the remains of the former Bull Yard premises where stored L.P.T.B. private hire coaches were destroyed during the Blitz. And the advert on the side of this RM has always puzzled me - it looks as if it refers to a sleepy Polish village, but Poland was behind the Iron Curtain then! Meanwhile, route 173 was renumbered P3 when converted to O.M.O. XA operation in January 1970.

The long and winding route 122, which at this period ran all the way from Crystal Palace to Bexleyheath, with a Saturday extension to Slade Green, was one of several that terminated at Crystal Palace Parade. On 2nd May 1971, RT1753 (AM) negotiates the roundabout at the top of Anerley Hill to return eastwards. This route converted to RM in April 1978, but then gained MDs, initially crew-operated, less than two years later. These in turn had given way to new Titans by mid-1983.

Route 184 was another of the many tram replacement services in South East London. Initially worked with RTLs, it received RTs in the summer of 1966. On 6th July 1971, RT2106 (WL) stands at its Brockley Station terminus in Revelow Road, one of a number of obscure stands in South East London side streets. By now the route only served the Embankment loop in rush hours and Elephant & Castle was its daily inner terminus. The route converted to DMS O.M.O. in October 1971 and was eventually withdrawn in 1994.

Route 234B was a one-bus Sunday-only service that operated in the late 1960s and early 1970s covering the Selsdon to Purley section of route 234, and then continuing to South Croydon Garage. On 27th May 1972, the lone FRM1 (TC) stands at its Selsdon, Farley Road terminus which was also shared with daily route 54.

The 172 was a replacement for Kingsway Subway tram route 35, originally running all the way from Archway Station to Forest Hill. In 1957, it swapped its southern section with the 171 and ran to West Norwood instead, originally terminating at the Thurlow Arms. This terminus was later changed to West Norwood Station, where on 1st September 1972, RM93 (Q) stands in Hannen Road. The 172 was brutally cut back and diverted to terminate at Kings Cross amid the 1982 "Law Lords" cuts, and withdrawn three years later. Ironically, today's route 172 serves much of the old 172's original routeing in the New Cross and Brockley area.

The George & Dragon pub at Farnborough was for many years a terminus on the edge of the Central Area in outer South East London, where route 47 from Shoreditch and route 51 from Woolwich met end-on. On 4th October 1972, RT3243 (SP) rests there before running home to its garage via Ruxley Corner on the latter. This RT was one of 34 which had recently been bought back from London Country to cover shortages. The 51 converted to RM in June 1976 and then DMS O.P.O. in May 1977, and was replaced at the latter date on the Orpington to Farnborough section by the 229 which exchanged southern termini with it. This lasted only until September 1982, when the 47 and 229 were cut back to Bromley Garage and Orpington respectively and both replaced by new route 261 which ran through Farnborough rather than terminating there.

For many years, the main terminus in Lewisham, serving several routes, was a one-way loop in Rennell Street behind the Odeon cinema. On 18th November 1972, RT2875 (NX) arrives there on the first day of new route 151, introduced to serve the new Ferrier Estate in Kidbrooke. This terminus was notable for having offside loading - something that would never be tolerated in today's "Health & Safety" regimes! A new bus station adjacent to the Southern Region railway station replaced this terminus in 1978.

XAs resettled from Stamford Hill and Tottenham Garages in North London were converted for one-man operation, and moved to Peckham and South Croydon Garages in the winter of 1969/70. Monday to Friday route 234 was one of their haunts, on which XA29 (TC) stands at Selsdon, Farley Road terminus on 29th December 1972. Three weeks later, DMSs took over this route prior to all XAs being exported to Hong Kong in the spring of 1973 and today route 234 no longer exists in this area.

On 19th April 1973, RT1152 (A) has just set off from trolleybus replacement route 154's Crystal Palace terminus at the top of steep Anerley Hill, bound for Morden. Of note is the trolleybus traction standard still in use for street lighting and as a bus stop behind it. This route converted to DMS O.M.O. three weeks later.

Back at Farnborough, RT3230 (TL) sets off on route 47 for the long trek to Shoreditch on 23rd September 1973, leaving a Sidcup RT behind on the 51 on the stand. At this time, the 47 was worked by Dalston, Catford and Bromley Garages, the latter often working Farnborough to Lewisham "shorts".

Another stand used for buses terminating in West Norwood was in Cheviot Road, opposite Norwood Garage. On 18th August 1973, RM2031 (N) has turned short on the 137 from the west at Crown Point, just up the hill, and accompanies all-over liveried RM783 (SW), curtailed on route 2. The latter route converted to O.P.O. in June 1986, whilst Routemasters soldiered on on the 137 until July 2004.

Above: The traditional southern terminus for route 36 was Hither Green Station, where buses ran around the block to terminate in Springbank Road beside the railway. On 23rd September 1973, RM1376 (PM) has just arrived there. The 36 group of routes were the first based entirely in South East London to be fully RM-operated, in early 1963, but converted to crew MD operation in the spring of 1976. RMs returned early in 1980, and the last surviving route of the group to retain them, the 36 itself, did so until January 2005.

Left: Another South East London terminus where buses ran around and stood in inner-suburban side streets was at East Dulwich, Goose Green where such routes as the 37, 176 and 185 were curtailed owing to late running. It also became the regular terminus for rush hour-only route 176A for a few months in the early 1980s. On 30th November 1973, RT2527 (AC) is impeded by selfish motorists as it terminates there. Exactly five years before, route 176 - yet another tram replacement service originally - had the distinction of being the last to have RTLs running through the West End, and in the spring of 1976 was the last to have an all-RT service serving it too when it converted to RM. O.P.O. conversion followed in 1984.

It was common practice in the 1960s and 1970s for RMs used on major trunk routes during the week to replace RTs or RTLs on lesser routes at weekends, when not so many buses were needed on their "home" routes. A typical instance of this was the 194B in the Croydon area, which gained them on Saturdays when the 12 at Elmers End Garage converted to RM operation in March 1973. They did not last long on the route, however: 30th November 1973, on which RM1069 (ED) stands at its Shurlands Estate terminus, was its last day of crew operation, O.M.O. DMSs taking over next day. The complicated 194 group of routes was never RM-operated otherwise.

There were two separate bus termini at Norwood Junction Station fifty or so years ago, one on its up side serving such routes as the 40, 75 and 196; and one on the down where routes 12 and 197 terminated. On 28th December 1973, RT4452 (TC) stands at the latter, about to work a "short" to Croydon, Katherine Street. This route also fell victim to the then supposedly all-conquering O.M.O. DMS a week later.

The busy town centre at Woolwich had four different bus terminal stands in the 1960s and 1970s. On 18th July 1974, RT2591 (TL) stands at what was referred to on route 75's blinds as "Woolwich Free Ferry" terminus, actually on Market Hill beside the C.E.G.B. power station. This and the nearby Woolwich Arsenal complex were prime targets for the Luftwaffe during the war, and bomb damage from that time is still evident behind the RT. The turning circle here was originally built for trolleybus routes 696 and 698 in 1935. Interestingly, routes 54 and 75 followed each other from Woolwich to Blackheath, and then took entirely different routes to and from Croydon. The 75 converted to DMS O.P.O. in February 1977.

A North London trolleybus replacement route which reached South East London was the 17, which had replaced the 517 and 617 in February 1961 running from North Finchley to Holborn, and then extended to supplement route 45 via Blackfriars and the Elephant to Camberwell Green, where RM377 (HT) has terminated at the rear entrance of Walworth Garage on 24th January 1975. Bizarrely, between 1966 and 1971, the 17 was extended on Sundays to replace the 45, giving a very long and circuitous route from North Finchley to South Kensington! The 17 received crew DMs the day after this picture was taken, and was withdrawn at the end of October 1978, replaced by an extension of the 45 to Archway. The situation was reversed in August 1985, when the 17 was reintroduced as an O.P.O. route. It still runs today between Archway and London Bridge Station via Holborn.

Illustrating the offside loading and alighting arrangements at the Lewisham, Rennell Street terminus, RT1850 (SP) works a "short" on route 21 from there back to its home garage on 21st February 1975, a week before the 21 converted to RM operation. O.P.O. would overtake it in February 1986, and although the route ventures no further south than Lewisham today, conversely it has in recent times regained part of its pre-war routeing north of Moorgate as far as Newington Green.

Nicely illustrating the Crystal Palace Parade bus terminus in the mid-1970s, RM443 (N) heads a line-up on the stand there on 17th August 1975, when route 2B ran all the way to North Finchley on Sundays. Behind it, the RT on route 122 has along trek ahead of it in the other direction, to Bexleyheath. Just visible between two RMs at the rear is an SMS, probably on route 227. Route 2B was eventually the last of the 2 group of routes to be Routemaster-operated, latterly renumbered as 2. It converted to O.P.O. in January 1994.

Petts Wood was another Southern Region railway station to have two separate bus termini. Short workings on route 94 turned at the western (up) side of it, whereas route 161A turned on the eastern (down) side. On 17th April 1976, RT2742 (AW) arrives at the latter terminus a year and a month before the 161A's conversion to RM operation.

I am dealing with the Croydon area in this volume only with routes that operated east of the town centre. Two of these, as mentioned above, were the 54 and 75 which reached Woolwich, and on 29th October 1977 a DMS on route 75 and RM762 (ED) both await departure for that point at West Croydon Bus Station. By this time, the 54 was RM-operated at weekends, though an RT from Catford is behind the RM on the route on this occasion. The 54 converted to DMS O.P.O. in April 1978.

Routes 40 and 40A had a complicated service pattern in the 1960s and 1970s. On Sunday, 2nd April 1978, at which time the 40 ran at weekends only and the 40A during the week, RM1213 (PR) sets down its last passengers as it terminates at the special stop for Norwood Garage in Ernest Avenue. At this time, Poplar RMs and Camberwell DMs (off route 172's allocation) worked it on Sundays. Three weeks later, the 40 was introduced daily using Poplar RMs and Camberwell RMs on weekdays and their DMs at weekends. It was also rationalised and combined with the 40A, which number was discontinued, and withdrawn south of Herne Hill, running daily to Blackwall Tunnel with a rush hour extension to North Woolwich. The inevitable conversion to Titan took place, initially crew, in 1984, then to O.P.O. the following year. Today, a much revised route 40 links Dulwich and Clerkenwell Green.

The new route 151 converted from RT to RM in January 1975, still sporting lazy blinds. On 21st April 1978, its last day of crew operation prior to DMS O.P.O. conversion, RM1798 (NX) stands at its Ferrier Estate terminus. Sadly, this new estate soon degenerated into a notorious blackspot for mugging, burglary, knife crime and so on and has since been demolished and replaced by "improved" social housing. Route 151 no longer exists, either.

Powis Street was another place in Woolwich where buses terminated and stood, notably the 51 and 161 group of routes. On 22nd April 1978, RM8 (SP) awaits the off on route 161 for Chislehurst as its crew appear to be advising a lady passenger which bus to take. This RM had been a "Chiswick Experimental" vehicle until only two years previously when it finally entered service after eighteen years. It was preserved when the 161 converted to Titan in the mid-1980s. The DMS behind it is on route 54's first day of O.P.O. and no doubt received a poor reception from all and sundry!

Although route 180 was the first outer suburban route in South East London to convert to RM operation, in October 1968, RTs continued to operate it as subs for almost another ten years. On 25th August 1978, their last day of operation from Catford Garage and the penultimate day of all RT operation in the area, a very careworn-looking RT4210 (TL) reverses onto the stand at Lower Sydenham Station. Shared with Abbey Wood Garage which replaced its RMs with crew-operated MDs in January 1981, the 180 converted to O.P.O. in August 1985, having latterly been operated by crew-operated Titans. Today it links Lewisham and Belvedere via Woolwich.

Busy trunk route 1 received a weekday extension from Lewisham to Bromley Garage in January 1965, replacing route 199. On 26th July 1978, RM1725 (NX) departs from the latter point to Waterloo. The route converted to O.P.O. in June 1987, by which time this extension had been cut back again and the 199 reintroduced.

At Eltham Well Hall Bus Station on 2nd September 1981, by which time workings on routes 161 and 161A had been combined as the 161, RM250 (SP) has turned short and accompanies a Leyland National on route 126. This had been an early conversion from RT to MB operation in the autumn of 1968.

A new bus station was opened adjacent to Lewisham Southern Region railway station in the spring of 1978, replacing the precarious facilities, or rather lack of them, around the corner in Rennell Street. On 13th October 1981, RM704 (SP) sets off on a short working of the 21 to its home garage, contrasting with two DMSs and an MD. The latter had by this time all been resettled at Abbey Wood and the old Plumstead Garage working local routes, and would move to the new Plumstead Garage at the end of the month. However, their reign there would be short - all were gone by the summer of 1983.

With Bostall Woods in the background, RM1584 (NX) departs from the old Plumstead Garage, to where route 53 was extended on Sundays from Plumstead Common, on 18th October 1981, the penultimate Sunday that this worked. RMs had returned to the 53 the previous January after four years of crew MD operation, and would be replaced by O.P.O. Titans in January 1988.

By 1st June 1982, RMs have replaced the RTs once so familiar at the Farnborough, George & Dragon terminus for more than five years, but would not remain much longer. Here, RM24 (TB) is going to run the short distance back to its home garage on the 47, whilst RM301 and RM741 (SP) are bound for Erith on the 229. The latter route fell to Titan operation amid the "Law Lords" cuts just three months later, with the same fate befalling the 47 in 1984. Additionally, the 47 was withdrawn south of Bromley Garage amid the "Law Lords" cuts and replaced by new route 261, which also replaced the 229 between Farnborough and Orpington.

West Croydon Bus Station, originally opened in January 1964, is in the throes of rebuilding as DMS1894 (ED) sets off from there on 29th May 1983, leaving one of its fellows on the stand on route 130B. By now, the days of these non-B20 DMSs were numbered, even though they were only eight or nine years old. The 130 group of routes and the related C routes serving New Addington will be featured in my "Roadside in South West London" volume.

B20 DMSs lasted somewhat longer at London's service than their predecessors, but only thanks to the penny-pinching policies of the Tory puppet L.R.T. regime installed after London Transport's destruction in June 1984. Recently overhauled in all-red livery, DMS2331 (BX) looks very drab as it departs from Lewisham Bus Station on the same day as the previous picture. These vehicles had replaced RTs on route 89 just over five years previously but would soon be replaced by Titans and transferred in the main to South West London.

As mentioned earlier, route 161 was jointly operated by Plumstead MDs and then Titans and Sidcup RMs in its last few years of crew operation. Of the latter, RM292 (SP) pulls out of Woolwich, General Gordon Place on 13th February 1984, leaving a Titan behind it on the stand there where such routes as the 54, 99 and 122A terminated.

Yet another obscure inner-suburban backstreet terminus in South East London was Rosendale in West Norwood, where RM1274 (SW) is one of two RMs which have terminated there on route 2's last day of crew operation, 20th June 1986. Previously route 2A during the week and route 172 on Saturdays had served this terminus.

Under The Bridges

Calling at Waterloo Station beneath the main line bridge taking Southern Region trains out of Charing Cross, Saunders-bodied RT4247 (NX) on route 1 is about to be overtaken by a "Red Arrow" MBA on 19th May 1969. The second bridge in the background once carried a track linking the London & South Western Railway terminus with the South Eastern & Chatham Railway's Waterloo East Station, but by now had long since been used merely as a pedestrian link between the two.

On 19th September 1970, RT2533 (BN) has just passed beneath the bridge at Bingham Road Station in Addiscombe Road, working route 50's Saturday extension beyond its usual Streatham Garage terminus to Addiscombe, Black Horse. It had been replaced at this end by new route 289 in June 1968, and would convert to DMS O.M.O. in July 1971. The bridge was said to be too low for either an RM or a DMS to safely pass beneath. The station was on the Selsdon to Elmers End branch of the Southern Region, latterly operated as a rush hour-only shuttle, and closed in 1983. However much of it was resurrected by Croydon Tramlink in 2000, and Addiscombe Station on that is at this point today, albeit using a level crossing rather than a bridge to cross the road.

The low railway bridges on the Southern Region Kent Coast main line at Beckenham Junction are the reason why route 227 has to be single-deck operated. On 5th December 1970, a packed RF403 (TB) illustrates how even an RF only just fitted beneath them. The route converted to SMS O.M.O. four weeks later, the 227 having been the penultimate crew-operated RF route.

Route 78, in its last couple of years of crew operation, used RTs during the week and RMs at weekends. On 7th March 1971, RM428 (PM) has just passed beneath the impressive railway bridge carrying the mass of Southern Region tracks out of London Bridge Station over Tower Bridge Road. DMS O.M.O. befell this route in May 1972.

A Southern Region local train composed of both Bulleid S.R. and B.R. Standard EPB units passes over the bridge at East Dulwich Station as RT897 (WL) heading for Lewisham on route 176 escorts one of its fellows on the 184 beneath it on 6th July 1971. The 176 was the last of the four ex-tram routes passing here (the others were the 176A and 185) to retain crew operation.

On 30th August 1972, RT1573 (TL) passes beneath the bridge at the Southern Region's Lee Station. At the time this was said to be too low for DMSs to pass beneath. However, the underside of the bridge was modified to allow them to do so, and the 75 succumbed to DMS O.P.O. in February 1977.

A high-ceilinged tunnel takes the Sevenoaks Road beneath Southern Region main line south of Orpington Station. On 18th September 1973, RT4526 passes through it on route 51A. Converted briefly to RM operation in the spring of 1977, this route was withdrawn in May of that year when the parent 51 converted to DMS O.P.O. and was diverted to terminate at Green Street Green, this making the number 51A superfluous. The 229 was diverted to Farnborough replacing the original 51 routeing.

Winter sunshine catches RT939 (TB) running home to Bromley Garage beneath the Southern Region main line railway bridges in Brookmill Road, Lewisham on 24th January 1975, two days before the 47 converted to RM operation. Close to this location is St. John's Station, where the dreadful railway disaster took place in December 1957, involving an express bound for the Kent Coast hauled by "Battle of Britain" class 34066 "Spitfire" running into the back of a crowded commuter EMU in fog during the evening rush hour, and the loco fouling the supports for a bridge carrying the Nunhead Loop over the main line, bringing it crashing down onto the wreckage. Ninety people died and many more were seriously injured.

On a wet 30th April 1977, three weeks before the 161 and 161A's conversion to RM operation, RT4426 (SP) passes beneath the railway bridge at the Southern Region's Eltham, Well Hall Station. The SMS heading in the other direction is probably on route 108.

Newly-overhauled RM1249 (N) is running in to Norwood Garage, perhaps as a result of a staff cut, when passing beneath the Southern Region main line at Herne Hill Station. At this time, route 68 ran from Chalk Farm to South Croydon, being operated by garages at these two locations as well as Norwood. It converted to O.P.O. in October 1986, and today is split into three overlapping routes, the 168 being the northern section, the 68 the central and the 468 the southern.

The short route 42 between Camberwell Green and Aldgate, which had once ventured beyond the latter point through the East End and Stamford Hill to Finsbury Park, or later, Turnpike Lane, had converted from RT to ex-Red Arrow MB O.M.O. in January 1970, and then to DMS three years later. However in November 1979 it lost these in favour of SMSs, by now on their way out. On a gloomy Sunday 9th December 1979, SMS556 (Q) has just passed beneath the railway bridge in Tower Bridge Road and calls at the stop at the junction with Tooley Street. DMSs returned to the 42 in July 1980, but just a few days later Titans ousted them! Today the 42's northern terminus is Liverpool Street Station and it is somewhat longer, continuing to East Dulwich in the south.

In Lewisham Road on 13th October 1981, RM1213 (TL) has just passed beneath the tracks leading from Lewisham Station towards Blackheath. In common with other routes at Abbey Wood Garage, their share of the 180 moved to the new Plumstead Garage at the end of the month using crew MDs, which had been supplanted by new Titans by the summer of 1983. O.P.O. conversion followed two years later.

At the western end of Lewisham Station, a packed RM764 (PM) passes beneath the railway bridge heading for West Kilburn (alias Queens Park Station) on route 36B on 14th September 1982. This route was subsequently withdrawn north of Victoria and converted to O.P.O. in March 1992, and renumbered 136 two years later. The "core" 36 retained RMs, eventually running between Lewisham and Queens Park, until January 2005.

The bridge at Lee Station has long since been modified to allow DMSs to run beneath it, as B20 DMS2491 (TL) heads for West Croydon on 12th March 1983. Titans replaced these DMSs in July, though a small Sunday allocation of them from Elmers End and then South Croydon Garages worked on the 75 later in the 1980s.

The long route 12 gradually got shorter during the 1970s and 1980s, being cut back at both ends. By 12th August 1988 when RML2469 (Q) heads along Penge High Street beneath the Southern Region Brighton main line at Penge West Station, its southern terminus was the Pawlene Arms a little further on, and its western one East Acton. The route retained Routemasters until November 2004, by which time it linked Notting Hill Gate and Dulwich, Plough. Conversion to bendibus saw it cut back in the west to Oxford Circus.

RMLs at Camberwell Garage for route 12 occasionally found their way onto RM-operated route 3, as RML2604 (Q) has done on 27th June 1992, having just passed beneath the railway bridge in Croxted Road, Herne Hill. This somewhat battered RML will soon be refurbished to keep it going for another twelve years in service, however route 3 converted to O.P.O. six months after this picture was taken.

The driver of RML2342 (N) seems amused as I snap his bus passing beneath the bridge carrying West Norwood Station over Norwood High Street on 26th January 1994, the last day of their operation on route 2. This version of the 2 was in fact renumbered from 2B only ten months previously, and a close look at this RML's number blind shows how the "B" has been blanked out. This RML typifies those refurbished during 1992-1994 and is an ex-London Country specimen.

Between 2002 and 2005, bendibuses seemed to be all rage in London. Not only were several important routes converted to them following their debut on Red Arrow services, but two new routes, the 436 and 453 - variations of the existing 36 and 53 - were introduced using them early in 2003. In May 2009, MAL106 (NX) departs from the latter's Deptford Bridge terminus, having just passed beneath the D.L.R. station bridge. Absurdly, the contract for this route changed in 2007, necessitating London Central to obtain a new batch of "07"-registered vehicles as illustrated here. Just two years later they were withdrawn and replaced by conventional O.P.O. double-deckers - what a waste!

A more durable new type of London bus around the turn of the century was the DLA, a low-floor DAF with Alexander ALX400 bodywork. In May 2010, DLA184 (TC) has just passed beneath the bridge carrying the railway line from Crystal Palace to Sydenham over Penge High Street on the by now much-altered route 197. Although no DLAs remain in service now, a few Arriva VLAs (Volvos) with similar bodywork remain in service at the time this book is being compiled.

Churches

An imposing church which is one of the first buildings encountered upon entering South East London is St. John's, just south of the roundabout at the southern end of Waterloo Bridge. At lunchtime on 4th November 1968, RT3485 (NX) passes it on its way to Marylebone on route 1. This has a Park Royal RT10 body, and by now the days of these vehicles were numbered.

On 10th February 1973, XA14 (PM) passes St. Silas' Church in Nunhead, at the junction of Ivydale Road and Merttins Road, shortly before being exported to Hong Kong and replaced by DMSs on route P3. I wonder if the nasty dents at the front were repaired first?

At exactly midday on 29th December 1974, RT3783 (TB) works the Sunday service 119B, passing the imposing Church of St. Mary the Virgin, which has been on this site in Hayes, Kent for more than 800 years. As for the 119B, it converted to RM operation (using vehicles newly allocated to Bromley for RT replacement on the 47) four weeks later.

Left: Eltham Parish Church of St. John The Baptist, on the corner of Eltham High Street and Well Hall Road, is a well-known landmark in the area, and also dates back more than 800 years. On 23rd February 1975, RT3283 (SP) passes it on its way to its home garage, a few days before route 21 converted to RM operation.

Below: Probably only well-known to locals was this church at the junction of Crescent Road and Burrage Road, Woolwich which RT1762 (SP) passes on route 51's last day of RT operation, 8th June 1976. The Elim Pentecostal sect are using it here, but apparently nowadays use different premises nearby. Meanwhile, route 51 converted to RM operation next day.

Beckenham Parish Church, St. George's, also dates back more than 800 years and on 27th September 1977, RT1620 (TL) hurries past it on route 54's long route from Woolwich to Croydon. This RT has special significance to me in that I did my conductor training from Chiswick on it in 1974. It had already been a trainer for best part of four years then, but was reinstated to service in March 1976, surviving for two years until withdrawn a few weeks before route 54's DMS O.P.O. conversion in April 1978.

On a miserable 19th January 1980, DMS209 (PM) arrives at the Dulwich, Plough terminus of route 78, which had received these vehicles in May 1972. Behind it is the parish church of St. Peter, dating from the 19th century and closed a few years after this picture was taken. It has latterly been taken over by a "happy clappy" sect apparently. DMSs were replaced by MDs just over a month after this picture was taken. They in turn gave way to single-deck Leyland Nationals at the end of October 1981, with Titans replacing them amid the Law Lords cuts of September 1982 and lasting for several years until the route's loss to London Buses upon tender. Today, the 78 still runs but from Liverpool Street to Nunhead.

In May 2009, bendibus MAL36 (NX) contrasts with the ancient Church of St. Mary of Ravensbrook as it sets off for Paddington. These contraptions were replaced by conventional O.P.O. double-deckers in November 2011, and few saw further service.

Pubs

On 10th May 1968, Saunders-bodied RT1272 (TC) rounds St. George's Circus, complete with a side or rear blind in its front via box and a badly set destination blind, which should read "South Croydon Garage". The Duke of Clarence pub on the right at this time had a rather unsavoury reputation for having strippers performing at lunchtimes, in a "cage" just inside the corner doorway, which was left open in hot weather thus they could be seen from the street! At this period, I was sometimes lured there by office colleagues, but, as the saying went at the time, I was only there for the beer! Meanwhile, route 68's RTs were to be replaced by RMs in February 1970, and the pub has been derelict since at least the 1980s.

Typifying bus termini in earlier times, the forecourt of The Black Horse at Addiscombe was the terminus of route 50, and then new route 289 which replaced it on weekdays in June 1968. On the latter, RT3902 (TH) departs for the short trip to Thornton Heath Garage on 3rd August 1970. The route converted to SMS O.M.O. at the end of October, and today is much longer, running from Purley to Elmers End. Sadly, the pub was closed in 2005 and demolished, with shops and flats above them occupying the site today.

In contrast, The Baring Hall pub at Grove Park is still going strong today. On 6th July 1971, RT160 (TL) - then the lowest-numbered RT in service - speeds past it on its way to Catford, St. Dunstan's College. The route converted to RM shortly afterwards, but then fell to O.M.O. DMSs in January 1972.

Many pubs adjacent to railway stations had the name "The Railway Tavern" as did the Courage house on the left opposite Slade Green Station. On 27th May 1972, RT2231 (AM) passes it as it arrives there on route 122's Saturday extension. This extension was withdrawn when the route converted to RM in April 1978. Sadly, the pub building was converted into "apartments" in 2006, having closed some time previously.

Another Railway Tavern which was also a Courage house was opposite Nunhead Station. Sadly, this pub too is now but a memory and flats occupy its site. However, at least initially, the pub sign was retained. In this view, XA14 (PM) still has its frontal dents when passing on the Nunhead loop route P3 on 16th February 1973.

For many years, Charrington's White Swan public house dominated the roundabout at the top of Anerley Hill, where on 23rd April 1973, RT833 (A) terminates on route 157, which had been extended here to supplement the 154 when it replaced trolleybus 654 in 1959. Both converted to DMS O.M.O. three weeks after this picture was taken. Alas, this pub too is no more.

Typical of Victorian pubs in inner South East London was the impressive Father Red Cap at Camberwell Green. Sadly, although it still exists it no longer serves real ale and now goes by the naff-sounding name of Nolleywood! In happier times, RT2056 (WL) on route 176 is pursued by an RM passing it on 10th May 1973. Bizarrely, this RT ended up some eight years later being abandoned at the roadside in Willesden by its new owners (who had attempted to convert it to a burger bar), and then towed away by gypsies and broken up.

42

On 14th September 1973, RM285 (Q) passes The Thurlow Arms at West Norwood, then an Ind Coope house, on tram replacement route 196, which had been withdrawn north of Euston in March 1971 and converted from RT to RM operation. In January 1974, it would be shorted to terminate at Brixton to where it was diverted from Herne Hill, then converted to O.P.O. in September 1982. Trams and then the buses that replaced them once terminated at The Thurlow Arms. Alas, this pub too is now kaput - a Tesco "Metro" store occupies its site today.

A landmark on steep Shooters Hill was Courage's pub The Bull when RT4422 (NX) passed it turning from Shooters Hill into Shrewsbury Lane on 4th October 1973. Fortunately, this traditional pub which dates back to 1749 is still flourishing today! Route 192, which linked Lewisham and the Woodlands Estate in Plumstead and served some very hilly territory in the area, converted to RM operation in May 1976 then to DMS in April 1978. It then converted to MD in September 1980 when transferred to the old Plumstead Garage, but was withdrawn when that closed at the end of October 1981, largely replaced by a new route 291.

At Lee Green on 17th April 1976, RT4033 (TB) is one of two on route 94 in this picture turning from Lee High Road into Burnt Ash Lane. This RT is one of the 34 reacquired from London Country in 1972. Somewhat confusingly, the pub on the left is called the Old Tiger's Head, whereas the one just visible on the right is called The New Tiger's Head! The latter closed in 2005, although flats above it are still in use and the building is listed locally, whilst the Old Tiger's Head is still going strong. As already referred to in these pages, route 94 was the last RT-operated route in South East London and converted to RM operation in late August 1978. It was withdrawn just over four years later as part of the "Law Lords" service cuts, with new route 261 replacing this section of it.

A few days before route 119's conversion to RM operation, RT3871 (TB) passes the ornate Hare and Hounds pub on the Purley Way in Waddon on 28th April 1976. Despite being on this busy trunk route, the pub is still there today. As for route 119, it converted to crew Titan in October 1984, progressing to O.P.O, the following spring. It still runs between Bromley and Croydon Airport today. RT3871 is still running too, as part of The London Bus Company's heritage fleet, one of the mainstays of the Epping Ongar Railway's route 339.

This busy rush hour scene at Blackheath Station sees RT2182 (BX) loading up on 19th April 1978, three days before route 89's conversion to DMS O.P.O. It is outside The Railway pub, then an Ind Coope house. This traditional pub is still thriving, too.

On Sunday 16th January 1983, RM2188 (PM) hurries through Vauxhall Cross on its way to Hither Green. The big queue of people behind the RM are waiting to get into The Royal Vauxhall Tavern, which opens at midday to the delight's of Adrella's "Sunday School", introduced to the strains of Joe Meek's "Telstar". Anyone for sweeties? This famous pub is still a firm favourite in the LGBT community and now a listed building.

Oddities

One of two roofbox RTs approaching Eltham, Well Hall Station on 28th May 1968, Saunders-bodied RT4249 (AW) running back to its home garage, Abbey Wood, on the 161A is one of just a handful of such vehicles given white fleet-names on overhaul in the summer of 1966. It also sports a nice upper-case front via blind.

The dreadful unreliability of the MB, SM and DM-types, coupled with a nationwide shortage of spare parts in the mid-1970s, led London Transport to hire a batch of Leyland Titan PD3s from Southend Corporation. These replaced RMs on route 190 from South Croydon Garage during the autumn and winter of 1975/76. On 9th October 1975, Massey-bodied Southend No. 338 (TC) arrives at Thornton Heath High Street terminus.

DMS unreliability also led to the reversion of route 132 at Bexleyheath Garage to SM operation in the autumn of 1979 for a few weeks. SM5 (BX) passes through Crook Log on 1st October that year. Route 132 had originally converted from RT to SM operation in April 1970.

DMS854 was the prototype B20 DMS, modified from a standard vehicle in 1974. The basic difference with these was that they were supposed to be quieter than the earlier examples, with cowls fitted above their engines. This may just be discerned on this one. The last 400 of the class (DM/DMS 2247-2646) were of this specification, delivered in 1977-79, and although they were just as unreliable as the rest of the class, lasted in service longer with the last being withdrawn in 1993. This view shows DMS854 in Eltham High Street on 2nd September 1981. It was withdrawn two years later, but along with many others of its class, saw further service in Hong Kong.

In 1983, Titan T113 (PD) was one of two given this special livery, redesignated TE113 and route-branded for an express version of route 177. Long after this service had ceased, it is still carrying the special livery when passing through Forest Hill on route 122 on 18th October 1976.

Also at Forest Hill Station, RV1 (SF) is a 1966 Park Royal-bodied A.E.C. Regent V new to East Kent that had been purchased by Leaside Buses for private hire work. On 11th March 1994, it specially works route 171 on its last day terminating here. The route was extended to Catford Garage next day.

Rainy Days

More than once when I bought a Red Rover ticket to travel around various part of London photographing buses, the rain set in. But I carried on regardless, and many of the pictures I took in rainy conditions have been said to be "atmopsheric". Perhaps that may be said of this view of Saunders-bodied RT252 (AW) heading along Market Hill, Woolwich on route 180 in pouring ran on 29th September 1967. Usually, Saunders-bodied RTs could be easily recognised by having had their offside route number stencil holders being set further back than those on other RTs. However, on this one, it has been removed and plated over.

On a dreary, drizzly 9th February 1968, RT1859 (NX), another Saunders, passes the Imperial War Museum in Kennington Road on tram replacement route 163's long journey from Plumstead Common to Parliament Hill Fields. It had been extended to the latter point from its original Victoria Embankment terminus in January 1965, but was totally withdrawn five years after that.

Torrential rain falls around RT3029 (AM) as it passes the Eardley Arms in Upper Belvedere on 22nd January 1970, two days before route 99 converted from RT to MB O.M.O. - the last route to do so using new MBs. In fact the first SMs, which superseded them, entered service the same day on route 160.

A shabby RT686 (AW) sloshes through the ran running back to its home garage on route 161A at Mottingham Station on 30th April 1977, three weeks before routes 161 and 161A converted to RM operation. Despite its appearance, this RT saw another eleven months' service at Plumstead Garage on route 122.

On the same day as the previous picture, RM383 (SP) stands at a rainy Eltham Well Hall Bus Station. This Monday to Saturday-only outer suburban route had been RM-operated on Saturdays since March 1975, using RMs off the 21's allocation, and converted fully to RM three weeks after this picture was taken. Their tenure was brief, however: it converted to DMS O.P.O. in January 1978 and the route no longer exists today.

12th May 1977 was another soggy day in South East London, as RT3016 (SP) heads along Elmwood Drive, Bexley on the original section of route 229. Along with the 161, 161A and 228, this route converted to RM operation nine days later, making quite an impact on the hitherto virtual monopoly of RTs on local routes in the Eltham, Bexley and Sidcup areas.

A battered-looking RT397 (TB) stands at the Bromley North Station terminus of route 146 after a spring downpour on 14th April 1978, eight days before route 146 converted from RT to BL O.P.O.

It is also a wet day in South East London as RT280 (TL) calls at Grove Park Station on route 94 on its way to Orpington on 14th April 1978, some four an a half months before this route converted to RM operation. Of note here is the cut-down bus stop, with its e-plates to the right of the stop flag, specially made to fit beneath the rather low station entrance canopy.

During the brief period when all surviving MD-class Metro-Scanias were concentrated at the new Plumstead Garage, MD149 (PD) heads into Woolwich Town Centre on a very wet New Year's Day 1983. Route 291 had replaced the 192 in this area on 31st October 1981, when the new garage opened.

On 11th September 1983, RM1138 (TL) accompanies Titan T582 (WL) laying over in a wet Lewisham Bus Station. New route 208 had replaced parts of route 94 in September 1982, whilst the Titan had entered service replacing DMSs the following month. Route 208 converted to crew Titan in June 1984, then to O.P.O. in February 1986. It still links Lewisham, Petts Wood and Orpington today. Similarly, tram replacement route 185 still links Lewisham and Victoria.

The first half of bendibus MAL38 (NX) is stuck in traffic outside New Cross Gate Station in torrential rain in March 2009, some six years after new route 436 was introduced. These contraptions were, by accident or design, often, as in this case, allocated to so-called "deprived" areas where surely commonsense should have dictated that they would encourage fare evaders, as they and the so-called "New Routemasters" have ever since with their three entrances and exits!

Substitutes

In London Transport days, and the early years of London Buses Ltd prior to route tendlering and privatisation, allocations of vehicle types to routes were very rigid and it was quite unusual to see, for instance, at RM operating a route usually worked by RTs, and vice-versa, at the same time as the other type (discounting, of course, RT-operated routes that had RMs at weekends with joint garage allocations). However this sometimes did happen, usually if the intended vehicle(s) for the routes in question were unfit. RTs, therefore, fairly often worked route 141 from New Cross Garage in place of RMs. On 20th March 1969, RT3548 (NX) subs for an RM when heading for Grove Park at St. George's Circus. RT appearances on this route were much more common during the mid-1970s spares shortage.

Route 159 had converted to RM operation in June 1970, after which appearances on the route by RTs were quite rare. However, on 30th October 1972, a smart RT4552 (AK) puts in an appearance opposite Lambeth Palace working short to Baker Street. At the time I took this picture, no one could have foreseen that this route would be the last to operate an all-day Routemaster service in London, as far into the future as December 2005!

Although RMLs were scheduled to replace RMs on route 68 at various times during the early 1970s, their appearance was in fact sporadic. However on 23rd March 1973, RML2745 (TC), one of those allocated for the 130 group of routes in the Croydon area, heads for home along Walworth Road. The 68 converted to O.P.O. in October 1986.

Route 68 converted from RT to RM operation in February 1970, and after that RTs from South Croydon Garage made occasional appearances on the route until removed from the garage in January 1974. However, on 18th August 1973 at least two of them were working the route, and this lucky shot shows RT3714 (TC) and RT3960 (TC) passing each other on Beaulah Hill, Norwood.

Also in Norwood, but in West Norwood High Street on 30th August 1973, RT2576 (SW) subs for an RM on route 2. Although RTs from Cricklewood had worked this route prior to replacement by RTLs at the end of 1962, they had never been allocated to it from Stockwell Garage, which had used RTLs until the route converted to RM in the summer of 1967. This RT was allocated to Stockwell for route 168.

A remarkable appearance just after Christmas 1973 was that of RT3925 (AR) subbing for an RM on route 171. This route had only been RT-operated from Tottenham Garage for just over three months in 1968, replacing RTLs and then being replaced by RMs. However by now, the vehicle spare parts shortage was beginning to bite, so it was sent there as a spare for RM cover, joined shortly afterwards by two others. On 29th December 1973, I travelled all the way from home in Canonbury to Forest Hill, where it stands at the 171's Westbourne Drive terminus. I travelled all the way back to Tottenham on it too, using up an entire 36 exposure film on this strange phenomenon. Equipped with RM side-blinds in the front via box, these RTs also found their way onto the 41, 76 and, rarely, 73 routes, but moved away in the spring of 1974. However, history repeated itself two years later when three RTs again appeared as spares at Tottenham, this time staying for over a year and also setting the scene for similar unscheduled RT allocations at several other garages.

Right: At the time this survey begins, route 35 was operated by Leyton RTs and Camberwell RTLs, the latter being ousted by RTs in the summer of 1966. The route then converted to RM operation upon being cut back from Chingford and Leyton to Hackney Station and diverted there via Cambridge Heath upon "Reshaping" in September 1968. During the mid-1970s spares shortage, RTs from Camberwell's allocation for route 172 occasionally subbed for RMs - on 1st February 1974, RT4811 (Q) heads south along the bus lane at Camberwell Green. Route 35 converted to O.P.O. in June 1986.

Below: Across the road at Walworth Garage, RTs allocated for the 176 and 176A also subbed for RMs on route 45, which had received them in replacement of RTWs in January 1966. On 7th February 1974, RT676 (WL) negotiates the roundabout at the junction of Newington Butts and Walworth Road, approaching Elephant & Castle.

Back at Camberwell Green, RT2556 (PR) subs for an RM on route 40A which was shared between Camberwell and Poplar Garages. It is from the latter's allocation for the 277A. That route was withdrawn in August 1976, as was the 40A in April 1978 upon the daily reintroduction of route 40.

A very notable substitute visiting South East London on 11th March 1977 is RT2506 (WN), one of three rogue RTs allocated to Wood Green Garage during 1976/77 as RM spares and used on both the 29 and 141. Working through to Grove Park by the 141's Wood Green allocation were quite sparse, thus this appearance of the RT at Brockley Rise is quite notable. The route converted to crew DM just over a week later. In more recent times, its southern section has been replaced by new route 172.

Although route 180 had been the first local route in South East London to convert from RT to RM, back in the autumn of 1968, RTs continued to sub for RMs on it for a long time afterwards. On 17th May 1977, RT1800 (AW) does so in Plumstead High Street four days before Abbey Wood Garage lost its RT allocation when route 161A converted to RM. It is in fact a Plumstead bus on loan to Abbey Wood.

Although route 47 had converted from RT to RM operation in January 1975, RTs continued to operate it from both Bromley and Catford Garages right up until their final withdrawal from South East London when route 94 gained RMs. On their penultimate day, 25th August 1978, RT449 (TB) speeds south through Bromley Common.

The only RMLs ever allocated to a garage in South East London prior to their appearance at Camberwell and Peckham Garages in the late 1980s/early 1990s were a handful at New Cross Garage for their small share of route 37. Occasionally, they subbed for RMs on route 53, and rarely, routes 1, 141 and 171. On 7th May 1981, RML2490 (NX) runs out from the garage to take up service on the 53 in the evening rush hour.

It was much more unusual for DMs to sub for Routemasters than vice-versa, but on 2nd June 1982, DM2587 (SW) passes through Tulse Hill in place of an RM on route 2B. It had been allocated to Stockwell Garage for route 168, but when that was withdrawn in April 1981 it remained there as an RM/RML spare until moved on briefly for tours and charter work.

Another instance of DMs subbing for RMs was that of those allocated to New Cross Garage for the 141 finding their way onto route 53. On 1st June 1982, DM1063 (NX) passes Lambeth North Station bound for Camden Town. The 141 reverted to RM operation for a couple of years at this period, putting an end to this spectacle, whilst the 53 converted to OPO in January 1988.

Somewhat rarer than their appearances on route 53 were those of New Cross RMLs on route 171. On 25th June 1983, RML2722 (NX) pulls away from the stop opposite New Cross Garage bound for Forest Hill. Just over three years later, this tram replacement route converted to Titan operation.

Destined to be London's last all-day Routemaster-operated route, the 159 as never fully RML operated, and before the route's cut-back to Streatham Garage in February 1987, their appearances on it were rare. A week beforehand, on 31st January 1987, a shabby RML2468 (BN) passes Kennington Church bound for the terminus at the junction of Streatham High Road and Green Lane. It was derived from route 137's allocation.

Diversions

A long term-diversion in the Elmers End area caused buses on route 54 to carry special canopy slip-boards in the latter part of 1967. On 17th December that year, RT1289 (TL) passes through Rushey Green, Catford on its long journey from Woolwich to Selsdon.

Route 54 was affected again in the autumn of 1970, this time by road subsidence in Blackheath Village. On 17th October, RT2151 (TL) heads along normally unserved Elliott Hill through Blackheath.

Route 75 was diverted for the same reason, with journeys from Croydon terminating at Lewisham, Rennell Street, a point the route did not normally serve. Also on 17th October 1970, RT3676 (TL) heads for it along Belmont Hill.

Extensive road "improvement" works (carried out by the G.L.C. department I "worked" for at the time, Planning & Transportation's Construction Branch) at Vauxhall Cross on 20th March 1971 necessitated a long diversion of bus routes that headed south over Vauxhall Bridge towards Kennington Oval and Stockwell, via Albert Embankment, Lambeth Road, Kennington Road and Kennington Lane. RT815 (WL) heads around the roundabout at the southern end of Lambeth Bridge on this. Tram replacement route 185 converted to DMS O.M.O. in May 1973.

Route 2 was also affected by this diversion, and also on 20th March 1971, RM40 (SW) heads along then then-unserved Kennington Lane. Buses on the 2 group of routes and the 88 had to turn right at the southern end of this road into Harleyford Road and then back to the southern side of the L.S.W.R. main line at Vauxhall to reach South Lambeth Road. Numerically, this RM is now preserved, and resides near the famous town of Llanfairpwllgwyngyllgogerychwyrndrobwllllantysiliogogogoch in North Wales!

Road subsidence struck again in the Blackheath area in the early 1970s, when huge holes appeared in busy Lee High Road. South- and eastbound buses had to be diverted, and on 30th August 1972, RT3817 (AM) turns from Belmont Hill into normally unserved Brandram Road, from where it would regain its normal line of routeing in Lee High Road.

Almost a year later, on 23rd August 1973, the Lee High Road diversion is still in force and not surprisingly since bus routes such as the 21, 94, 122, 151 and Green Line coach route 719 were diverted along residential Brandram Road, residents were up in arms. With a background of slogans on fences and walls, RT3783 (TB) is one of two that do appear to be speeding along it!

A blockage in Stamford Street, Waterloo on 7th March 1977 has resulted in routes 70, 76 and 149 having to be diverted between Blackfriars Bridge and Waterloo via Blackfriars Road and The Cut, into which RM787 (SF) turns on the latter route. Today, Southwark Station on the Jubilee Line stands at the location on the left of this picture, with a subway connection to Waterloo East Station on the main line out of Charing Cross, which passes over the bridge behind the RM. At the time this picture was taken, the 149 was allocated crew DMs, but inevitably RMs had to sub for them.

Maintenance work on Tower Bridge caused routes 42 and 78 to be diverted via Tooley Street and London Bridge on 10th May 1980. MD90 (PM), one of the ill-fated Metro-Scania Metropolitans, passes London Bridge Station on the latter.

School Buses

As elsewhere in the London Transport system, some routes in South East London worked special journeys for schoolchildren. Of note were the journeys on route 54 that were extended from its usual southern terminus at Selsdon to Riddlesdown for this purpose. It is obviously the "lull before the storm" as RT1380 (TL) awaits its passengers there on 20th October 1972 on a purpose-built turning circle.

On 12th May 1977, schoolgirls clamber aboard RM851 (SP) in Alma Road, Sidcup, to where short workings on routes 51 and 51A ran for their benefit, as well as journeys on route 94 extended up from Orpington. The offside loading is of note. Route 51 converted to DMS O.P.O. nine days after this picture was taken.

Also in Sidcup on the same day, RT1312 (SP) turns from Central Parade into Hatherley Crescent packed with schoolchildren as an RM on route 51 heads south. Route 51's conversion to O.P.O. and the associated 51A's withdrawal nine days later enabled RM's to replace all remaining RTs at Sidcup Garage, on routes 228 and 229. The latter was withdrawn north of Bexleyheath Garage daily, except for a rush hour extension to Erith. New DMS-operated route 269 covered the Woolwich to Bexley section.

Also for the benefit of schoolchildren, short workings on route 54 ran between Croydon and Beckenham Junction Station, where a battered RT489 (TL) waits on 27th September 1977. The masking on its via blind box is a relic of when it was an RM spare at Tottenham Garage early in 1974.

Back in Alma Road, Sidcup, RT3351 (TL) has arrived with the very last RT-operated school journey on route 94, on Friday, 25th August 1978. As may be observed, there was a fixed bus stop for these journeys, but buses usually stood on the other side of the road, as illustrated above.

Across The Tracks

Buses in South East London crossed many bridges over Southern Region railway lines. On 11th May 1972, two days before route 78 converted to DMS O.M.O., RT918 (PM) crosses the tracks leading into Bricklayers Arms Goods Depot on Dunton Road, Bermondsey. The nearby motive power depot had closed with the demise of steam in the early 1960s, and the goods depot would soon follow suit.

On 19th April 1973, RT2788 (TL) crosses the railway bridge at Catford Bridge Station, and will shortly pass beneath another bridge at nearby Catford Station in Catford Road, on route 75's trek from Woolwich to West Croydon. The proximity of these two stations, on different branches, typifies the complexity of former Southern Railway commuter lines in South London.

There were few level crossings in South East London that affected bus routes, but one of the busiest was at Abbey Wood Station. On 12th October 1974, RT4726 (AW) crosses it when subbing for an RM on route 180, and is one of the 34 RTs repurchased from London Country two years previously. Not long after this picture was taken, the level crossing was replaced by a bridge in connection with the development of the new Thamsemead estate nearby.

On 11th October 1978, RM2043 (TB) crosses the bridge at Waddon Marsh Station on route 119's rush hour extension to Thornton Heath Garage via the Purley Way. At the end of the month, this routeing was altered and the 119 no longer crossed this bridge, running to Thornton Heath High Street via London Road instead. Today, Croydon Tramlink has replaced the Southern Region West Croydon to Wimbledon branch through Waddon.

On 13th November 1983, B20 DMS2386 (ED) crosses the Southern Region Brighton Main Line at East Croydon Station, on route 194 which had initially converted from RT to SMS in October 1970. Today, a Croydon Tramlink interchange with the main line station on this bridge has radically altered the scenery here.

The New Order

The "New Order" under London Transport's ill-fated Reshaping Plan at first saw few incursions into outer South East London by new one-man operated vehicles, perhaps explaining why RTs ruled the roost there for so long. However, MB-types did reach the area in late October 1968 when they replaced RTs on routes 21A, 108 and 126, and RFs on route 202 (the latter becoming new flat-fare routes P1 and P2). On 22nd January 1970, 50-seat conventional O.M.O. MB306 (SP) sets off from Eltham, Well Hall Station for Farningham on the 21A. Two days later, the shorter SM-types also first appeared in the area working routes 160 and 160A. Neither the MB nor SM-types lasted very long, mainly through their notorious unreliability, but also because they were in effect rendered obsolete when one-man operation was permitted on double-deckers.

Sadly, the first mass-produced one-man operated double-deckers built for London Transport, the DMSs, were just as unreliable in service as the MB and SM-types, which in many cases they replaced, instead of replacing RTs as intended. By 3rd September 1982, when DMS1860 (BX) passes Sidcup Police Station on route 269 which had replaced the northern section of route 229 in May 1977, they were already on their way out and mass withdrawals of non-B20 DMSs took place next day amid the "Law Lords" cuts.

The final batch of DMSs, the supposedly quieter B20 types, lasted somewhat longer than their predecessors, but only really because of the penny-pinching policies of the Thatcher regime's London Regional Transport puppet, who tried to get their money's worth out of them. On 19th June 1983, one of these, DMS2510 (TL) calls at Falconwood Station on route 160, which had initially converted from RT to SM O.M.O. in January 1970. It was replaced by Titans soon afterwards.

From late 1978 onwards, even when the last DMSs had only recently been delivered, London Transport had given up the ghost with them, and both M.C.W. Metrobuses and Leyland B15 Titans were replacing them, starting in West and East London's outer suburbs respectively. By the time of the "Law Lords" cuts, most surviving DMSs ran in South London and L.T. carried out comparative trials with Metrobuses and Titans at Sidcup Garage to see which was the best type to replace the DMSs there. With a badly set destination blind, M805 (SP) passes through Orpington on 21st April 1983.

Initially, Leyland B15 Titans were chosen to replace DMSs in South East London, and the small batch of Metrobuses at Sidcup migrated north of the Thames. Typifying the new order of the early 1980s, Titan T830 (SP) stands at a wet Lewisham Bus Station on 11th September 1983.

As will be illustrated in full later, Titans also replaced the short-lived MD class Metro-Scania Metropolitans which briefly comprised the entire allocation of the new Plumstead Garage when it opened at the end of October 1981. One of these, T679 (PD), stands in for one of the specially-liveried Titans used on the 177 Express service at Waterloo roundabout on 6th June 1984.

Titans also briefly replaced Routemasters working as crew vehicles in South East London, before the routes involved inevitably converted to O.P.O. under the L.R.T. regime. Route 180 was an example of this, on which T855 (TL) turns into Southend Lane, Bellingham on 26th October 1984. Of note is the "Pay Conductor" flap beneath the windscreen, and the conductor may be discerned standing next to his driver. LS-class Leyland Nationals were also used at this period in South East London, usually to replace MB or SM-types on routes restricted to single-deck operation, but also, bizarrely, to replace RMs on recently-introduced route 261.

Ordered before the destruction of London Transport by the Thatcher regime in 1984, but delivered in bulk after it, the L-class Leyland Olympians were in some ways a progression of the Titan and continued in production for London Buses into the 1990s. Most of them were based in South London, and replaced the last of the DMSs. Equipped with "split-step" entrances, they survived into the present century before the "all-low-floor" diktat enforced their withdrawal from London's Streets. On 8th June 2002, L47 (TH), which has pinched RM47's registration, approaches East Croydon Station on route 198, effectively a renumbering of the former 194B.

Metropolitans

A class of London bus unique to South East London was the MD class Metro-Scania Metropolitan. Delivered from late 1975 until early 1977 and envisaged as a replacement for the unloved DMSs, 164 of them were built and all initially were used as crew-operated buses, perpetuating the current trend of doored buses (hitherto a crew version of the DMS termed DM) displacing RMs which in turn replaced RTs elsewhere. The 36 group of routes at Peckham Garage received them in the spring of 1976, followed by the 63 there in the autumn. On 25th March 1976, new MD3 (PM) passes the old Peckham Town Hall a couple of days after entering service.

The remaining MDs entered service at New Cross Garage on route 53 during January 1977. Four years later, on 2nd January 1981, a battered MD149 (NX) approaches the Charlton, Hornfair Road terminus of this route, at which it is unusually curtailed. The route reverted to RM operation at the end of the month, the 36 group having already done so a year or so previously. By this time, all of the class had become early candidates for withdrawal owing both to heavy fuel consumption, and a tendency towards corrosion of their all-steel bodywork.

Apart from any seriously damaged in collisions, etc, the MDs were retained, more or less, until their seven year certificates of fitness expired and when displaced by RMs were either farmed out to outer South East London garages Abbey Wood and Plumstead or kept at Peckham for O.P.O. route 78. At first, they replaced RMs on routes 161 and 180 at Abbey Wood and 122 at Plumstead, retaining conductors. MD20 (AM) exemplifies the latter, complete with "Pay Conductor" flap, when changing crew in Wickham Lane, Plumstead on the last day of the old garage there's operation, 30th October 1981. In effect, MDs from the 36 group of routes had been exchanged with the 122s RMs in January 1980.

Somewhat peculiarly, route 63 at Peckham Garage held on to its MDs working as crew-operated buses until the "Law Lords" cuts of September 1982, when RMs finally replaced them. On 30th October 1981 too, MD91 (PM) approaches the junction of Old Kent Road and Albany Road.

Also on the same day as the previous picture, MD63 (AM) crosses Blackheath on route 192, where MDs had replaced DMSs when its operation was transferred from New Cross to the old Plumstead Garage in September 1980. This was the 192's last day of operation; it was in effect renumbered 291 (involving minor route alterations) next day when the new Plumstead Garage opened.

30th October 1981 was also the last day of Abbey Wood Garage, which along with Plumstead had become a 100% MD garage early in 1980. On that final evening, MD116 (AW) sets off for the last time on an evening rush hour spreadover duty on route 272. This route had been introduced originally with DMSs in November 1974, to serve the growing new Thamesmead development. The route was withdrawn in January 1999, with a new route 472 replacing it.

Another route in the Woolwich area operated by the short-lived MD class was the 122A, which had converted from RT to MB operation in the summer of 1969, then graduated to DMS and then MD operation. On 3rd September 1982, MD123 (PD) calls at Woolwich Arsenal Station with an RM on the 53 bringing up the rear. This route was withdrawn in January 1988, largely replaced by a new route 422.

On 14th September 1982, the same MD as in the previous picture has just departed from Waterloo heading for its home garage on route 177. Following the 63's reversion to RM operation ten days previously, routes 78 and 177 were the only services on which MDs were scheduled to work into Central London - but not for much longer.

Route 178 was another which had been introduced to serve the new Thamesmead development, initially being the outer section of the 177 east of Woolwich renumbered when introduced in September 1980. On 27th October 1982, MD35 (PD) approaches Woolwich town centre, with the high wall on the left protecting the Woolwich Arsenal complex from prying eyes. Today, a much altered route 178 links Woolwich with Lewisham via Kidbrooke.

A little further to the East than the previous picture, MD82 (PD) also approaches Woolwich on a short working of the 161 on the same day. Of note is that this MD, one of those moved a few weeks previously from the 63, has no "Pay Conductor/Driver" flap at the front, and is still crew operated. Its conductor, complete with Gibson ticket machine, is clearly visible beside his driver. Sidcup RMs still co-worked the 161 at this time.

On New Year's Day, 1983, MD108 (PD) is one of three different types of O.P.O. double-decker in evidence at Plumstead Station. Of note is the "Pay Conductor" flap - route 180 was still crew-operated too at this time, shared with Catford RMs. But the MDs' days are numbers, and one of the new Titans being delivered to the new Plumstead Garage is on route 178 behind it. A B20 from Bexleyheath Garage on route 269 brings up the rear.

MD127 (PD) was the last of the Metropolitans in service, and on the occasion of an open day at the new Plumstead Garage on 25th June 1983, it put in a farewell performance giving a tour of local routes that they had operated. It departs from the garage with a full load of passengers, passing the replacement Titans, of which T676 has been working route 161, still with a conductor.

Double Take

It was not that often, especially in South East London where RTs dominated the scene for so long, that two different classes of bus could be seen together working the same route in the 1960s, 1970s and 1980s. Nevertheless, it did happen. Busy trunk route 53 had converted from RT to RM in the autumn of 1967, but RTs based at New Cross Garage still subbed for RMs on it for several years afterwards. At the route's Plumstead Common terminus on 9th August 1971, RT2875 (NX) accompanies one of the scheduled RMs.

This scene in the grounds of Bexley Mental Hospital on 19th September 1971 is very odd indeed, since routes 124 and 124A never ran together! The 124 was the weekday service, running from Forest Hill to Welling, whereas the 124A was its Sunday variant which went to Bexley Hospital instead. Clearly, the RT, RT2559 (TL), is really working the 124A when accompanying RM1290 (TL). The two routes converted from RT to RM operation in late July 1971, but then went DMS O.M.O. in early January 1972, thus making them one of the shortest-lived scheduled RM operations of all.

Route 197 was one of many which had an RM allocation at weekends, but never received them daily. On 10th February 1973, a Saturday, RT2036 (TC) has been fielded on the route instead of one of the scheduled RMs, one of which follows it in this extremely rare scene in Morland Road, Lower Addiscombe. The route converted to DMS O.M.O. in January 1974.

An exception to the general rule of two different types of bus working the same route at the same time on a scheduled basis was that of the 36 group of routes, when they were converted gradually from RM to MD operation in the spring of 1976. Thus RM1387 (PM) and MD22 (PM) stand side by side at Lewisham Obelisk on 17th April that year. At first the MD's were well-received by passengers and staff alike, being nicer looking, more comfortable and more reliable than DMSs. Corrosion and heavy fuel consumption was their downfall.

Both the 161 and the 180 has joint RM and MD crew operation in the early 1980s. On 2nd September 1981, RM113 (TL) speeds past MD142 (AW) on the latter route in Lewisham Road, Greenwich. Eventually, both types were replaced by Titans.

Following the MDs' demise, Titans also worked routes 161 and 180 alongside RMs in the early/mid-1980s until O.P.O. conversion obliged Titans to replace the RMs. On 23rd June 1983, RM250 (SP) overtakes a Titan on route 161 approaching Eltham Church on one of its rush hour journeys to Charlton.

Suffixed Routes

Suffixed routes were usually either deviations from their "parent" routes, or weekend and sometimes rush hour variations of them. There were many in South East London. Of the former, route 21A operated the outer end of the 21 beyond Sidcup Garage to Farningham on Mondays to Fridays, and also had a rush hour extension to Woolwich from its usual inner terminus of Eltham, Well Hall Station. On 28th May 1968, RT782 (SP) arrives at the latter point a couple of weeks before the route was withdrawn north of Sidcup Station. It then converted to MB O.M.O. at the end of October 1968.

Route 228A was a Monday to Friday variation of the 228 which ran from Chislehurst to Eltham and Greenwich, but continued to Blackwall Tunnel, South Side rather than to Surrey Docks Station as the 228 did. On 15th July 1968, Saunders-bodied RT1922 (SP) calls at Blackheath, Royal Standard heading west. It is one of just a handful of these RTs to receive an experimental white fleetname on final overhaul in the summer of 1966, and also sports a nice upper-case via blind. The 228A was withdrawn at the end of October 1968 when the 228 itself was cut back to Eltham, Well Hall Station.

Route 1A was a Sunday variation of the 1, introduced in January 1967, and terminating at Greenwich Church rather than Lewisham or Bromley at its eastern end. On 9th March 1969, RT2726 (NX) stands at its Greenwich terminus bound for Willesden Garage. The route converted to RM operation a week later, was withdrawn north of Charing Cross in October 1969 and then completely nine years later. However, it reappeared briefly in the mid-1980s until the 1 itself was rerouted to Greenwich, rendering the "A" redundant.

Originally, route 108A was a variant of the 108, starting at Bromley-by-Bow and then continuing alongside it through the Blackwall Tunnel to Greenwich, from where the 108 continued to Crystal Palace and the 108A to Eltham. Following the single-decking of the 108 owing to the height restriction in the northbound tunnel at the end of October 1968, the 108A was rerouted away from it to continue to Surrey Docks Station during rush hours and on Saturdays, and London Bridge Station in the early morning on Saturdays, and also converted to RM at weekends. On 20th September 1969, RM1751 (NX) is about to cross Blackheath. The route was withdrawn in January 1970.

Route 194, which linked Croydon Airport with Forest Hill, had three variations fifty years ago - the 194A, 194B and 194C. The 194A ran on Mondays to Saturdays from Beckenham Junction to Croydon, with a rush hour extension to Thornton Heath Garage. On 27th September 1969, a smart RT4619 (ED) heads along Addiscombe Road into central Croydon. This route was withdrawn, along with the Sunday variant 194C which also ran from Croydon Airport to Forest Hill but with a different routeing from the 194 in the Shirley area, when the 194 converted to SMS O.M.O. at the end of October 1970. The 194B remained crew-operated for another three years.

Route 141A was introduced as a weekend service in November 1961 in conjunction with route 141's replacement of trolleybus route 641. It was in fact tram replacement route 179 renumbered, and ran from Grove Park up to the City, then all the way to Finsbury Park. A long extension of the 141 on weekdays from Moorgate to Grove Park replaced the 179 then. It was co-worked by Holloway (J) RTs and New Cross RMs, of which RM552 (NX) rounds the Elephant & Castle roundabout on 19th October 1969 working to Highbury Barn only, as it did by now on Sundays. A week later, the Sunday service was withdrawn, and the route ceased altogether when the old Holloway (J) Garage closed in September 1971 and route 4 was reintroduced daily to cover the Finsbury Park to City section, and the 141 extended to Grove Park at weekends.

A Sunday variation of route 160, numbered 160A, replaced route 180 on Sundays on the section between Catford and Lower Sydenham. On 4th January 1970, RT4285 (TL) pulls out of Brownhill Road at Rushey Green heading for that destination. Along with the parent 160, this route converted to SM O.M.O. three weeks later.

Sunday-only route 188A was introduced in November 1964 in an effort to cut costs and combat staff shortages. It covered the Archway Station to Holborn Station part of route 172, and the Holborn Station to Greenwich part of route 188, both of those routes being withdrawn on Sundays. It was operated by RTs from Holloway (J) Garage and RTLs from Camberwell Garages, the latter replaced by RTs in the summer of 1966. On 14th March 1972, RT4802 (Q) stands at its Greenwich Church terminus with the famous Cutty Sark making a nice backdrop. The 188A was withdrawn a fortnight later upon the SMS O.M.O. conversion and reintroduction of the 188 on Sundays. The 172 was likewise reintroduced that day between Archway and Bloomsbury, but retaining RTs.

Introduced originally in October 1960 on Mondays to Fridays to localise the southern section of route 108 between Blackwall Tunnel South Side and Crystal Palace, the 108B became a daily route eight years later when the 108 converted to MB O.M.O. and was diverted to terminate at Eltham. Then, in January 1970, the 108B was extended to Surrey Docks Station in rush hours to replace the 108A. On 14th April, RT2005 (TL) collects passengers in Rotherhithe Old Road on the latter extension three days before the route converted to SMS O.M.O. Graduating to DMSs and then to Titans, it was withdrawn in November 1991.

Numerically a sister bus to the RT in the previous picture, RT2006 (J) passes The Chandos pub in Brockley Rise on 3rd July 1971, two months before what was by now Saturday-only route 141A was withdrawn, on its long trek from Grove Park to Finsbury Park.

Over the years, the 59 and 159 group of routes had a variety of suffixed variations, the last being the 59A. Latterly running from West Hampstead to Streatham Garage and using RTs on Mondays to Fridays, it was converted to RM operation at the end of October 1970, but severely reduced to run only during rush hours and between Charing Cross and Streatham, Telford Avenue. On 8th March 1972 shortly before its complete withdrawal, RM187 (Q) approaches Vauxhall Cross in the morning rush hour. The modern office building behind the RM is Camelford House.

Running from Thornton Heath High Street to Shrublands Estate in Shirley via central Croydon, route 194B was the last survivor of the 194's derivations. On 31st August 1972, RT4442 (ED) calls at Thornton Heath Station. The route gained RMs on Saturdays upon the 12's conversion to the type in March 1973, but converted to DMS O.M.O. the following December. It was renumbered 198 in March 1992.

In the same area, route 197A was introduced at the beginning of November 1970 as a variation of the 197, running in a horseshoe shape between Norwood Junction and Thornton Heath via central Croydon on Mondays to Fridays. On Friday 11th May 1973, its last day of RT operation, RT2149 (TH) heads along Portland Road, South Norwood with an SMS on route 12A in pursuit. Conversion to DMS O.M.O. took place the following Monday and the route was withdrawn in October 1978.

Route 161A was a variation of the 161, which it followed from Charlton Station (rush hours) or Woolwich (otherwise) to Chislehurst War Memorial and then continued to Petts Wood Station rather than Sidcup Garage as the parent 161 did. However, on 18th September 1973, RT4172 (AW) turns short at the war memorial, which a lot of buses on both routes did, as another RT coming from Sidcup on the 161 passes by. The two routes converted to RM operation in May 1977, and were combined as the 161 in September 1980.

The meandering route 119, which ran from Bromley to Thornton Heath via Croydon, was given a Saturday variation numbered 119A and a Sunday one called the 119B at the end of October 1970, all using RTs. The 119A's routeing between Croydon and Thornton Heath differed from the 119 by going via London Road instead of Purley Way, and it replaced the 194A on that section. On 17th April 1976, RT370 (TB), subbing for an RM to which the route had converted in March 1975, is about to turn from George Street, Croydon into North End. This route was withdrawn in October 1978 consequent upon the 119 taking over its routeing to Thornton Heath and being reintroduced on Saturdays.

Representing route 161A's spell of RM operation between May 1977 and its withdrawal in September 1980, RM222 (AW) is at the roundabout at the junction of Well Hall Road and Westhorne Avenue in Eltham on 6th April 1978.

Sunday-only route 119B differed from the parent 119 by diverging briefly in the Shirley area via Shirley Way to replace the 194C. On 29th May 1983, RM6 (TB) appears to be abandoned at a request stop in Westmoreland Road, Bromley but is in fact changing crew. The outgoing driver appears to have left his nearside direction indicator flashing, whilst a young lad consults the bus stop panel to see when the next moving bus is due! The route, along with the parent 119, converted to crew Titan in October 1984, but did not last long with these, since in April 1985 the Shirley Way section was replaced by a "new" route 194A, and the 119 reintroduced daily.

Interchanges

Most bus routes in South East London served Southern Region and London Underground stations. One that no longer exists today was Eltham Park, on which RT2063 (TL) calls on 22nd January 1970, two days before route 160 converted to SM O.M.O. This station, along with Eltham Well Hall, closed in conjunction with the inward extension of the M2 motorway, both being replaced by a new station mid-way between them named Eltham.

RT4793 (NX) is one of three RTs serving the East London Line's Surrey Docks Station on 14th April 1970. Route 70 was unique in being the only tram route to retain its number when replaced by motor buses. Six days after this picture was taken, the Monday to Friday only route converted to SMS O.M.O. Later graduating to DMSs and then Titans and for a while LSs, it was withdrawn in November 1988. Meanwhile, the station had been renamed "Surrey Quays" to reflect the yuppification of the former docks area a few years previously and is today served by London Overground trains.

War damaged buildings are finally being swept away as RT3443 (Q) approaches Elephant & Castle Station, served by the Bakerloo and Northern Lines, on 17th March 1971, ten days before route 188, another tram replacement, converted to SMS O.M.O.

On 11th December 1971, RT4539 (ED) is overheating as it pulls away from the stop on the bridge at Woodside Station in Spring Lane. This Southern Region station closed in 1997, but its site was reused for Croydon Tramlink which opened three years later, although the station buildings on the bridge remain derelict and boarded up. Route 12's section in this area was withdrawn between Norwood Junction and South Croydon Garage and replaced by new SMS-operated route 12A in January 1972.

Route 12 also served Forest Hill Station, at which RT3415 (PM) has just called on 3rd October 1972 when running back to its home garage. The long and winding 12 underwent a protracted RT to RM conversion between February and May 1973, and today no longer ventures south of Dulwich. London Overground as well as Southern trains serve Forest Hill today.

I was travelling around South East London on my 25th birthday, 27th December 1972, and one of my ports of call was Nunhead Station, where XA25 (PM) deposits passengers on Nunhead Circular route P3. Of note is the very nasty dent on its front offside. In the spring of 1973, all the XAs were exported to Hong Kong and replaced by new DMSs.

A couple of weeks before routes 154 and 157 converted from RT to DMS O.M.O., RT3581 (AL) has just called at Selhurst Station on the Brighton main line into Victoria on 27th April 1973. On the left is the Southern Region's extensive Selhurst Depot, situated in the V-junction between the main lines to and from London Bridge and Victoria, and a Bulleid EPB unit just noses in on the left.

As illustrated earlier, Norwood Junction station had a bus terminus either side of it, and on 21st October 1973, RM242 (PR) sets off on route 40's Sunday service to Blackwall Tunnel from the terminus on the up side of the station. On the stand, another RM on the same route accompanies one working Catford Garage's Sunday allocation on route 75, which terminated here that day rather than continuing to Croydon.

On 17th November 1973, RT803 (TL) nears the end of its long journey from Woolwich to West Croydon as it passes East Croydon Station. The monstrous tower block on the right is now one of several disfiguring the skyline here and, of course, the station is even busier today being also an interchange with Croydon Tramlink services.

Back at Surrey Docks Station, on 21st February 1975 RM403 (TB) illustrates the new order on route 47, which had converted from RT four weeks previously. Of note is the antique "Tickets and Trains" sign on the wall, which was presumably trashed when the station was rebuilt in the 1980s.

Shortly before the 36 group of routes converted from RM to MD operation, RM1552 (PM) passes beneath the bridge at Queens Road, Peckham Station on 21st February 1976. Today, this station is served by the revived link from Surrey Quays taking London Overground trains through inner South London to Clapham Junction, as well as Southern services.

A large crowd of people attempt to board RM974 (SP) at Sidcup Station in the evening rush hour of 12th May 1977, not helped by the selfish idiot who has parked a car right on the bus stop! Until the road under the railway bridge in the background was dipped to allow double-deckers through in the early 1960s, single-deckers had to be used here, latterly RFs. Route 51 converted to DMS O.P.O. nine days after this picture was taken.

Route 171 was another which served Forest Hill Station, for many years its southern terminus. On 6th April 1978, RM1542 (NX) has just arrived there at the end of its long journey from Tottenham. Today, this tram replacement route ventures no further north than Elephant & Castle!

Today, Beckenham Junction is one of the termini of Croydon Tramlink but on 20th April 1978, it was firmly in the hands of British Railways Southern Region. RM401 (TL) has just arrived there on a school journey of route 54, subbing for an RT. The route converted to DMS O.P.O. two days later.

Grove Park is a busy station on the main line to the Kent Coast, and also the terminus of the shuttle service to and Bromley North. On 1st June 1982, RM49 (TB) calls there offering an alternative means of transport to Bromley North just over three months before route 94's withdrawal. The dwarf bus stop beneath the station canopy illustrated earlier is still in place: I wonder if anyone ever pinched its e-plates?

On 25th June 1983, B20 DMS2443 (BX) has for some reason turned short at Plumstead Station, where it stands prior to return east. The flag of the bus stop tells how this is also an alighting point for buses terminating at the nearby garage.

Working short to Putney, RM1023 (NX) carries a very full load as it passes North Dulwich Station on route 37's last day of Routemaster operation, 20th June 1986. This once long inner suburban peripheral route which ran from Peckham to Hounslow, was wrecked by being cut up into three overlapping sections when converted to O.P.O. next day.

Moving ahead into the present century, Arriva Plaxton Pointer-bodied Dennis Dart PDL132 (N), one of the last of many hundreds of these buses built for London, typifies those used on outer London suburban routes in the first decade of this century. In August 2010, it crosses the bridge at Sydenham Station on route 450, which was introduced in 1993 linking Crystal Palace and Purley, but has subsequently been altered to run between West Croydon and Lower Sydneham. As the sign on the bridge says, this station is served by Southern and London Overground trains, the latter having been introduced there the previous May.

One a very familiar sight all over London when low-floor double-deckers were first introduced at the end of the last century, few buses with Alexander ALX400 bodies remain in service at the time of writing. Typifying them, Arriva Volvo VLA106 (N) departs from its Anerley Station terminus in September 2010 on a short working to Streatham of route 249, which has its origins in replacing the eastern section of route 49 in May 1971. Anerley is another station served by local Southern services and London Overground.

Sunday Service

In the days before Sunday trading was allowed, far fewer buses ran on Sundays, therefore RMs often replaced RTs on suburban routes on that day when not needed for their weekday routes. A typical example was route 197, running from Norwood Junction to Caterham Valley. On 26th November 1967, newly-overhauled RM1399 (TC) turns from George Street into North End, Croydon shortly before the 130 group of routes, for which it was allocated, converted to RML.

There were also a number of routes which ran only on Sundays (and sometimes on Saturdays too) that varied from weekday routeings. Usually they had a suffix letter, and typical of these was the 63A. It differed from the parent 63 by running to Hampstead Heath rather than Parliament Hill Fields at its northern end at weekends. On 17th December 1967, RM1441 (PM), still in original condition and soon due for first overhaul, passes its home garage on a quiet Sunday. This weekend route was withdrawn when the 63 was cut back to Kings Cross in January 1970.

Originally running throughout from Turnpike Lane to Farningham, by the late 1960s route 21 only ran south of Sidcup Garage at weekends (replacing weekday route 21A) and had been withdrawn north of Moorgate during the war. On 18th February 1968, RT3827 (SP) pulls away from the stop opposite Sidcup Garage bound for Farningham, and bears a lazy via blind usually carried by the 21A. The following June, this extension was withdrawn upon the weekend introduction of that route.

Route 122A usually ran only between Erith and Woolwich, but had a very long Sunday extension paralleling the 122 all the way to Crystal Palace. On 9th March 1969, RT835 (AM) has worked that section, as its via blind shows, when on the daily part of its route at Plumstead Corner. The extension was withdrawn when the route converted to MB O.M.O. in July 1969.

Route 160A was a Sunday variation of the 160, which replaced the 180 on Sundays between Rushey Green and Lower Sydenham and also continued beyond the weekday 160's Welling terminus to Plumstead Garage. On 4th January 1970, RT4285 (TL) passes through Falconwood, where it replaced route 124 on Sundays too, to the latter point three weeks before the route converted to SM O.M.O. It later received DMSs and was withdrawn in April 1978, but reappeared in a slightly different form between 1982 and 1985.

As referred to earlier in these pages, route 194C was a Sunday variant of the 194 to which it had a different routeing in Shirley. Also on 4th January 1970, RT2864 (ED) stands at its Forest Hill Station terminus. The route was withdrawn at the end of October that year when the 194 converted to SMS O.M.O. and was replaced on its Shirley bifurcation by the 119B.

From the November 1958 route cuts until April 1970, route 40 ran all the way from Wanstead Station to Norwood Junction Station on Sundays, latterly using Upton Park RMLs. Sister buses RML2511 and RML2512 (U) keep RM1231 (TL) on the 75 at the latter point company on 4th April 1970, a fortnight before this service was cut back to Poplar.

An oddity on the Sunday-only 188A, as well as the weekday 188, was that since there was no right turn from Tower Bridge Road into Tooley Street, buses had to turn left into narrow Fair Street and circumnavigate the block of Victorian flats, turning right into Tooley Street and then going straight across the junction. On 7th March 1971, RT4811 (Q) undergoes this manoeuvre three weeks before the 188A's withdrawal. Today, a bus-only right turn is in place here, and the old flats have been smartly refurbished and must now be worth a fortune!

The 124A was another Sunday-only route that terminated at Forest Hill Station, from which RM1060 (TL) sets off for Bexley Hospital on 24th October 1971, during the 124 and 124A's short-lived period of RM operation.

On the same day as the previous picture, RM967 (NX) passes the main entrance to Woolwich Arsenal on the Sunday-only 171A. Introduced in January 1966 to replace the Sunday 163A between Abbey Wood and Camberwell Green, and then the 171 all the way to Tottenham, this route was withdrawn six years later and replaced by a Sunday 180A which will be illustrated later.

This interesting scene outside Hayes (Kent) Station on 21st October 1973 captures two Sunday workings together. RT811 (TB) arrives on the Sunday-only 119B which had been introduced three years previously, as RT4772 (SP) has terminated on one of the odd Sunday afternoon journeys extended there on route 51. This RT was subsequently exported to Canada, but repatriated a few years ago to join The London Bus Company's Heritage Fleet.

On the same day as the previous picture, RM1203 (TL) sets off from Norwood Junction Station on this Sunday working of the 75, which was otherwise RT operated and converted to DMS O.P.O. in February 1977. The driver has forgotten to change his destination blind, but presumably it is bound for Blackheath, where the route terminated on Sundays rather than continuing to Woolwich.

On a cold, crisp 29th December 1974, RT4469 (TB) begins the climb up Corkscrew Hill four weeks before the Sunday 119B converted to RM operation following that type's replacing RTs on route 47.

Woolwich town centre is almost deserted as RM743 (AW) turns from Powis Street into Greens End at the start of its journey to Chislehurst on 23rd March 1975. The 161 from both Abbey Wood and Sidcup Garages had converted from RT to RM operation on Sundays three weeks previously, upon the 21's conversion to the type at the latter. Daily conversion followed in May 1977.

Also in Woolwich on a quiet Sunday, 4th July 1976, RM1618 (NX) heads along Market Hill heading for its home garage. The 180A covered the Plumstead to Abbey Wood section of the 180 via Abbey Estate - hitherto covered on Sundays by routes 177A, then 163A and then 171A - as far as Greenwich Church, and then paralleled the 177 as far as New Cross Garage, being shared by that establishment and Abbey Wood. It was withdrawn amid the April 1978 "Busplan '78" changes.

Route 51's Sunday extension to Hayes Station ran along roads otherwise not served by red buses, one being Croydon Road through Keston Common where RM851 (SP) heads along on 24th April 1977. The 51 had converted to RM operation in June 1976, losing them to DMS O.P.O. three weeks after this picture was taken, when this extension ceased.

A remarkable route to see Routemaster operation was the 146, running from Bromley North Station to the village of Downe, which however is well within the London Borough of Bromley. Allegedly owing to difficulties turning O.P.O. buses around the tree on the left of this picture of RM295 (TB) at the Downe terminus on 9th October 1977, RTs were retained until April 1978, but when Bromley Garage received RMs for route 47 in January 1975, these worked the 146 on Sundays. Just one bus was deemed sufficient! The final solution to the route's O.P.O. problem was using BLs to replace the RTs in April 1978.

Withdrawn in October 1978, Sunday-only route 1A was reintroduced in April 1984, running between Charing Cross and Greenwich, Cutty Sark and operated by New Cross RMs, as before. On 26th August 1984, RM744 (NX) sets off from Greenwich on its way back to the garage. This working was very short-lived, since the route converted to Titan O.P.O. in October, but was withdrawn just over a year afterwards when the 1 was diverted to terminate daily at Greenwich, thus obviating the use of the suffixed number.

Rush Hour

An odd case of a route which ran almost entirely within East London, but which also had short journeys mostly within South East London, was the 10. Running at its full length from Abridge via Woodford, Stratford, Bow and Aldgate to London Bridge, and then on via Borough, Elephant & Castle and Lambeth Bridge to Victoria, it had rush hour "shorts" between London Bridge, where RTL327 (BW) stands on 4th December 1967, and Victoria. The RTLs were replaced by RTs on "Black Saturday", 7th September 1968, and then the route converted to DMS O.M.O. in October 1972, which ensured its lingering death!

Many other routes had rush hour extensions. One was the 21A, which was extended from Eltham, Well Hall Station to Woolwich. On 28th May 1968, RT960 (SP) has come from Woolwich when passing beneath the bridge at Well Hall Station, a couple of weeks before this extension was withdrawn and the route cut back to Sidcup Station.

One of few instances of an entire route which ran during Monday to Friday rush hours only in South East London was the 176A, originally a tram replacement route. This followed the 176 from Lewisham to Elephant & Castle, then instead of heading for the West End, continued via Southwark Bridge to terminate at Cannon Street. On 17th September 1970, RT476 (WL) heads along Newington Causeway in the evening rush hour. The route converted to RM operation in March 1976, was withdrawn south of Dulwich in 1981, and totally the following year. Latterly, its City terminus was altered to become Mansion House Station.

Heavy rush hour traffic has always been a bugbear to buses. On 25th September 1970, RT4712 (ED) is stuck in it on the Purley Way when bound for Croydon Airport five weeks before the 194's conversion to SMS O.M.O. This RT is now part of the L.T. Museum collection.

Full buses are also a bugbear to rush hour passengers! In a remarkably traffic-free Blackfriars Road in the evening rush hour of 31st August 1971, a packed RT4109 (WL) leaves a big crowd standing at the bus stop as it heads south on tram replacement route 184. Converted to DMS O.M.O. the following October, this route has long since vanished from the South East London scene.

Heading south along Borough High Street in the evening rush hour of 26th October 1972, route 10's penultimate day of crew operation, RT3200 (BW) is one of the 34 London Country RTs bought back by London Transport to cover shortages a month previously. Masking tape has been used for a makeshift repair on its front via blind glass!

On a number of occasions, my by then ex-employer, the Greater London Council's Department of Planning and Transportation, tried their best to alleviate rush hour traffic congestion by "improving" Vauxhall Cross junction. Thus all appears to be a shambles on 8th May 1973 while works are progressing. RT3676 (TL) has been turned short there, and is running back to Catford Garage in the evening rush hour, "tipping out" at Rushey Green. The route converted to DMS O.M.O. three days later, no doubt adding to traffic congestion in the area as the things lumbered their way south from Victoria!

For the benefit of workers at the nearby dockyards and factories, several bus routes which usually terminated in Woolwich were extended eastwards to Charlton Station during rush hours. On 18th July 1974, RT2853 (AW) stands there. The "box" behind it is a DMS on route 96, and another RT is arriving on the 51A.

Odd rush hour journeys on route 229 were scheduled to terminate at St. Mary Cray Station, as RT3408 (BX) is doing in Hatherley Crescent, Sidcup on the route's last day of RT operation, 20th May 1977. RMs took over next day working from Sidcup Garage only.

Another route extended to Charlton Station in rush hours was the 51A, on which RM597 (SP) quite remarkably has Woolwich Church Street all to itself in the evening rush hour on 13th May 1977. Having only gained RMs in the latter half of January 1977, route 51A was withdrawn a week after this photograph was taken, thus making it one of shortest-lived RM allocations ever.

On route 149's brief foray into South East London, DM1058 (SF) disgorges passengers in York Road, Waterloo on 18th August 1980 in the evening rush hour, eight days after refurbished RCLs began to oust these contraptions from this route. Today, the scenery here has changed radically, with the Shell offices on the left replaced by new residential tower blocks.

In its later years, route 36A ran in rush hours only. On the evening of 20th July 1981. newly-overhauled RM420 (PM) approaches Camberwell Green with what looks like a full load of passengers bound for Brockley Rise. The route was withdrawn ten years later.

By 1983, the awful DM and DMS types were well on their way out. On 12th March that year, DMS2266 (TL) lumbers its way along Westhorne Avenue in evening rush hour traffic between Eltham and Catford. However, B20s like this one lasted a little longer than standard DMSs and it survived until 1991.

Routemasters dominate the scene at New Cross Gate in the evening rush hour of 21st June 1983, as RM1172 (PM) heads for West Kilburn on route 36. This would be the last route to operate them here, succumbing to O.P.O. in January 2005.

Hills

Parts of South East London are very hilly. This is typified by this view on 3rd October 1972 of RT1892 (TL) climbing London Road out of Forest Hill past the impressive Horniman Museum some five months before the 185's conversion to DMS O.M.O.

Anerley Hilll is one of the steepest in the whole of London, and in common with those climbing Highgate Hill in the north, trolleybuses (on route 654) that traversed it had to have special "run-back and coast brakes" to prevent them running backwards out of control in the event of a power failure. On 19th April 1973, with the North Downs as a distant backdrop, RT1107 (A) nears replacement route 154's Crystal Palace terminus at the top of the hill three weeks before this route also converted to DMS O.M.O.

Another steep hill route 185 had to negotiate was Dog Kennel Hill in Dulwich, a place always associated with the trams it, and the 176, 176A and 184 which also served it, had replaced. On 10th May 1973, RT2206 (TL) climbs it on the route's penultimate day of RT operation.

A climb on the four routes mentioned with the previous photograph heading south along Lordship Lane, East Dulwich was involved too. Also on 10th May 1973, RT483 (WL) heads for Forest Hill, passing one of the many local government housing redevelopment schemes in progress at this period which were quite often still replacing housing that had been damaged or destroyed during the World War Two blitz.

Passing one of the radio and TV transmitter masts in the hilly Crystal Palace area, RM1263 (Q) heads up the steep climb at the junction of South Norwood Hill, Church Road and Beulah Hill at Beaulieu Heights on 18th August 1973. Route 196 was yet another tram replacement route which had converted from RT to RM operation in March 1971. In January 1974, it was diverted at Herne Hill to terminate at Brixton Police Station, the section between Norwood and Euston being entirely duplicated by route 68. O.P.O. conversion followed in September 1982.

There are a number of hilly roads in the Woolwich and Plumstead area, too. RT3780 (NX) heads down steep Sandy Hill Road in Woolwich on the 192's tortuous route between Lewisham and Plumstead, Woodlands Estate on 4th October, as a cyclist walks his bike up the hill in the opposite direction. Route 192 converted to RM operation in May 1976, then to DMS O.P.O. just under two years later. It was subsequently withdrawn and largely replaced by new route 291, as related earlier.

Mention has been made before in these pages of Corkscrew Hill in West Wickham. A few days before route 119's conversion from RT to RM operation, RT4583 (TB) is about half way towards the summit on one of its twists and turns on 28th April 1976. It was often necessary for passengers to alight from buses climbing this hill in snowy weather and help their crews push them up it!

There are a number of hills on the southernmost edge of the former Central Area in South East London too. On 8th June 1976, RT2732 (SP) climbs steep Farnborough Hill three days before route 51's conversion to RM operation. Oddly, it seems to be missing a canopy number blind.

Just over a week before route 192's conversion to DMS O.P.O., RM1594 (NX) is a bit further down Sandy Hill Road, Woolwich than the RT illustrated above. The date is 14th April 1978 and this view illustrates just how steep this suburban residential road is.

Shooters Hill, on the old A2 from London to the Kent Coast, is another of South East London's most famous steep hills. On 21st April 1978, RT2484 (BX) is overheating slightly as it reaches the summit on route 89. Next day, O.P.O. DMSs took over this route, and as they used to when standing at stops or traffic lights, I shudder to think how they coped with this long, steep hill which the 89 shared for most of the way with the 192, which also received those contraptions next day!

Mason's Hill is to the south of Bromley town centre, and on 17th August 1978, RT4210 (TL) heads down it bound for Lewisham just over a week before route 94 finally converted fully to RM operation, this ending the operation of RTs in South East London.

The use of RMs on most local routes in South East London was short-lived, partly because RTs remained in use on them for so long and partly because many were converted to crew MD operation in 1980, and then to Titan. On 14th September 1978, RM955 (AM) on the 122 and RM38 (AW) on the 161A climb out of Woolwich towards Shooters Hill along Woolwich New Road. Both routes would converted to crew MD in 1980 and be transferred to the new Plumstead Garage the following year.

The area around Coulsdon on the northern edge of the North Downs is very hilly, too. On 17th September 1978, RM671 (AK) descends Meadway from Sunday-only route 59's Old Coulsdon terminus on its long journey to distant West Hampstead. This long-standing Sunday route was withdrawn five weeks later upon Sunday introduction of routes 159 and 190 which it had replaced and linked on Sundays.

In May 1977, route 229 took over the 51's previous routeing between Orpington and Farnborough and thus the Farnborough Hill section. On a bleak 2nd January 1981, RM311 (SP) nears its summit. The 229 converted to Titan operation amid the "Law Lords" cuts of September 1982.

The only RMs to be allocated to the Dog Kennel Hill routes on weekdays were those on the 176 and 176A. On 20th August 1982, RM100 (WL) reaches the summit on route 176, which had been the last route to retain scheduled RT operation through the West End when it converted to RM in the spring of 1976.

The DMS following RM100 up Dog Kennel Hill in the previous picture is DMS2113 (TL) on route 185. Two things are of particular note here. Firstly, a strap saying "No Entry" is clearly visible inside the DMS behind its entrance. This is to bar off the Automatic Fare Collection machine on the nearside - these were seldom used by passengers and their turnstiles were always jamming anyway! However barring it off impeded passengers boarding, making DMSs even slower in clearing queues than they were anyway. Secondly, the front advertisements are blanked out. This was because the swingeing cuts resulting from the "Law Lords" ruling against the Greater London Council's cheap fares policy were due to be implemented in a couple of weeks' time, and this DMS - only six years old - faced withdrawal as a result. Withdrawn it indeed was, though it did see eight years' further service with Grimsby Cleethorpes Transport.

On 14th September 1982, RM288 (TL) speeds down Masons Hill towards Bromley town centre on new route 208, which had replaced much of route 94 following its withdrawal ten days earlier as a result of the cuts. It covered the 94 between Orpington and Bromley, but then supplemented the 47 by running directly from Bromley to Lewisham via Catford, rather than via Grove Park and Lee, which new route RM-operated route 261 did instead. That route somewhat oddly converted to LS O.P.O. in the spring of 1983, but the 208 kept its RMs until June 1984 when crew-operated Titans replaced them, with OPO following early in 1986.

Routes 47 and 208 encountered Bromley Hill north of Bromley town centre, too. On 20th August 1984, RM818 (TB) speeds down it bound for Shoreditch. Titans took over this route too shortly after this picture was taken.

Crystal Palace sits at the top of Gypsy Hill, with all bus routes approaching it having a steep climb. On 4th September 1985, RM693 (PM) climbs Sydenham Hill nearing the terminus, three years after route 63 reverted to RM operation from MD. It converted to Titan O.P.O. just two months later.

Another very steep hill on the old A2 is Blackheath Hill, which RM1753 (NX) crests on 28th June 1986. Route 53 too had reverted from MD to RM operation in January 1981, but fell to Titan O.P.O. seven years later.

Roofboxes

Roofbox-bodied RTs perpetuated a body design dating back to the late 1920s, i.e having the route number box on the front dome of the body. About a quarter of the RTs were delivered with bodies carrying them, which were widely dispersed throughout the RT number range during overhaul, and by the time the survey in this book starts around a third of those bodies were still in service, some of them on RTLs. On a snowy 9th December 1967, Saunders-bodied RT3844 (TB) approaches Bromley North Station on route 94.

23 of the 27 RTLs which carried roofbox bodies were overhauled in 1964/65, all being RT10 types formerly on RTs and surviving until their final year in service. On 26th January 1968, RTL384 (PR) passes Surrey Docks Station and by now had the oldest body still in use. In common with Poplar's other RTL-operated routes, the 82 which traversed Rotherhithe Tunnel, received RTs to replace them on "Black Saturday", 7th September 1968. The route was withdrawn without replacement just seven weeks later.

All but a handful of the 350 Saunders-bodied RTs, all with roofboxes and the last to be delivered, survived to have a final overhaul 1965/66, with the last withdrawn early in 1971. Also on 26th January 1968, RT3182 (TB), another of these at Bromley Garage, heads along North Street, Bromley working route 126 which converted to MB O.M.O. at the end of October.

The original Gothic-styled Catford Town Hall at Rushey Green contrasts with its modern extension as Saunders-bodied RT3513 (WL) passes by on route 185's somewhat circuitous trip from Victoria to Greenwich Church on 18th February 1968.

Back in Bromley again on the same day, RT4394 (TB), another Saunders, changes crew in the High Street just north of Bromley South Station on a West Croydon-bound 119. This view shows clearly how Saunders bodies for some reason had their offside route number stencil plate holder placed further back than on other RT bodies, on which it was flush with the rearmost lower deck offside window. They were taken out of use in late 1963

Roofbox RTL1328 (BW) has just been reinstated after being delicensed at Cricklewood Garage and transferred to Bow when crossing the junction of Lambeth Road and Kennington Road on 10th April 1968, when working route 10's South East London incursion between London Bridge and Lambeth Bridge.

On the offside-loading stand behind Lewisham Odeon in Rennell Street, Saunders-bodied RT1727 (TL) has been curtailed there on a working of route 47 to Stamford Hill on 15th April 1968. The route had been extended there from Shoreditch in July 1961 to supplement the replacement of trolleybus route 647 (which, by coincidence, had replaced tram route 47!) but the extension was cut back again in January 1970.

Just around the corner on the same day, RT1879 (AM), another Saunders, heads along Lewisham Grove on route 122's long journey through the South East London suburbs from Slade Green and Bexleyheath to Crystal Palace.

Further to the East also on 15th April 1968, RT3595 (NX) passes the crossroads in Eltham High Street by Eltham parish church on route 21's trek from Sidcup, or perhaps Farningham on a Saturday at this time, to London Bridge. This has a Park Royal RT10 roofbox body dating from 1948, the oldest type now on RTs and next in line for withdrawal once the RTLs have gone.

Also in Eltham High Street, but on 4th May 1968, RT3102 (TL) is working route 124 bound for Forest Hill. Once the RTLs had all been withdrawn, at the end of November 1968, routine withdrawals also began of Saunders-bodied RTs, although this one survived into 1970.

On 21st May 1968, time is running out for RT10-bodied RTL98 (AR) which calls at Waterloo Underground Station in York Road on its way from Forest Hill to Tottenham; just over three weeks later RTs released from the withdrawal of route 182 at New Cross Garage replaced route 171's small allocation of RTLs at Tottenham Garage. Interestingly, this entrance to the Underground station was within the Shell Centre, and was mothballed when much of it was demolished in recent years. It has since been reopened beneath a new residential block on the same site.

Another elderly RT10-bodied RT serving the Eltham area in the spring of 1968 is RT2857 (SP) which calls at the stop opposite Eltham Church in Well Hall Road on 28th May, heading for its home garage at Sidcup on route 161.

On the same day as the previous picture, RT352 (TB) turns off Well Hall Road to terminate at Well Hall Station on route 61. Equipped with a nice set of upper-case via blinds, this Saunders-bodied RT was transferred to Cricklewood five months later when route 126 converted to MB O.M.O., replacing RTLs there. Its side advert is of note, mimicking RM front blind displays. Route 61 converted from RT to DMS O.M.O. in the summer of 1972.

On 9th July 1968, RT2243 (J) passes Kennington Church on tram replacement route 172. It carries an RT10 body and at this period, most surviving roofbox RTs with cream waistbands were of this type, since the majority of Saunders-bodied RTs were overhauled after grey waistbands were adopted in April 1965 and only a few which had been done at the start of their overhaul sequence in March of that year had cream ones.

Also at Kennington Church that day is Saunders-bodied RT4251 (Q) on weekday route 59A, whose routeing between this point and Lambeth Bridge differed from the 159 by going via Harleyford Road, Vauxhall Station and Albert Embankment, rather than via Kennington Road and Lambeth Road.

Blackwall Tunnel routes 108 and 108A were only RT-operated through the tunnel between 7th September (when they replaced RTLs) and 25th October 1968, the 108 converting to MB O.M.O. next day and the 108A being diverted away from the tunnel. Ten days beforehand, Saunders-bodied RT1581 (PR) approaches the Ship & Billet pub in Greenwich bound for the 108's weekday terminus of Lower Sydenham.

Back at Kennington Church, RT3756 (NX) is another RT10 based at New Cross Garage, and works tram replacement route 163 on 1st April 1969. Outrage was caused when this route, which ran on weekdays from Parliament Hill Fields to Plumstead Common, was withdrawn completely in January 1970.

Evening shadows lengthen as RT4247 (NX) approaches Woolwich, Beresford Square on 5th April 1969 on route 177, another tram replacement route. A second roofbox RT follows on route 99, both having Saunders bodywork.

In the summer of 1963, a small allocation of RTLs moved into the former Highgate Trolleybus Depot for route 196, whose northern terminus at Tufnell Park was a short distance from it. These were replaced by RTs two years later, and one of these, RT4040 (HT) passes the Old Vic Theatre in Waterloo Road on 13th May 1969. This had been a Country RT numerically prior to receiving a Saunders body upon overhaul in red in 1965. When route 196 converted to RM operation in March 1971, it was cut back to Euston and the Highgate allocation consequently withdrawn.

A close look at RT2469 (AW) shows that it has had its offside route number stencil holder removed and panelled over, making to difficult to recognise as being Saunders-bodied. It escorts an RF on route 227 working a Petts Wood-bound 161A journey through Chislehurst Common on 20th September 1969.

On 22nd January 1970, Saunders-bodied RT1844 (TL) arrives at route 160's Welling, Springfield Road terminus. Two days later, this route was the first to receive the new SM type in place of its RTs amid a series of route changes and cuts throughout London. These resulted in the last RT10-bodied roofbox RTs being withdrawn (although one was reinstated briefly at Thornton Heath Garage in early February), and also major inroads were made into the ranks of Saunders RTs - including this one. More were withdrawn as a result of route changes in April and June, with just a handful surviving after that. The last, RT1903, survived until March 1971 - outlasting all others thanks to having been fitted with saloon heaters, apparently in error, upon last overhaul.

Contrasts

On 24th March 1969, Saunders-bodied RT1888 (NX) contrasts with Red Arrow MBA191 when turning from The Cut into Waterloo Road. Both have just left the Cornwall Road bus stand, now used as the base for surviving Red Arrow routes, and represent one of the oldest and one of the newest buses in the London Transport fleet at the time. Route 70 had been cut back from Victoria to Waterloo when the Red Arrows in this area were introduced amid "Reshaping" on 7th September 1968.

On 17th January 1970, RM178 (D) working Dalston Garage's weekend allocation of RMs on route 47 through to Stamford Hill escorts an MBS on route P1 along Rotherhithe Old Road. The P1 had replaced route 202 in October 1968. The 47's extension north of Shoreditch was withdrawn a week later.

Beauty and the beast? The famous RT1702 (TL) contrasts with an SMS on route 188 when working route 1 to Bromley Garage at the southern end of Tower Bridge Road on Christmas Eve 1971. When new, this RT had toured northern Europe to promote the 1951 Festival of Britain, and always retained its original body on overhaul. When withdrawn in 1972, it was purchased by a group of busmen at Catford Garage and preserved. It remains in immaculate condition today and is probably one of the best-known surviving RTs, a great credit to its owners!

Certainly "beauty and the beast" in my book! At Bromley Garage itself, RT1383 (TB) has just terminated on 1st September 1972, as a new DMS loads up behind it on route 61, which had received these awful contraptions six weeks previously.

Illustrating how front entrance, rear engined buses could look attractive, XA36 (PM) on route P3 contrasts with RT3937 (ED) in Rye Lane, Peckham on 16th February 1973 during route 12's long-protracted conversion from RT to RM operation.

On Sunday 4th October 1973, the market stalls are absent from Woolwich, Beresford Square as all-over advertisement liveried RM783 (NX) escorts an RT and an MB across the tram track still in place in the cobbles more than twenty-one years after the last trams had run here. The RT has its via blind down and is running dead to Abbey Wood Garage off route 161. The MB, based at Plumstead, is working either the 99 or the 122A

Crossing Blackheath on 8th February 1977 on route 75 which will convert to DMS O.M.O. later in the month, RT248 (TL) makes an interesting contrast with a new MD which has recently entered service on route 53

Running around the block from Hare Street into Woolwich High Street to reach its Powis Street stand on 13th May 1977, RT549 (SP) contrasts with a DMS approaching on a short journey of the 177, which had received this type in place of RTs in January 1972. The 161 received RMs daily just over a week after this picture was taken.

Four different types of London bus are visible in this scene at Bromley North Station as RT4712 (TL) heads for Orpington on 27th September 1977. On the right is London Country AF8 (GD), one of the small batch of Daimler Fleetlines which had replaced RMLs on route 410 early in 1972, whilst two DMSs and a little BS class E.C.W.-bodied Bristol LH bring up the rear. The BS is working route B1, which had originally had Ford FS-class minibuses.

On 12th March 1983, RM1331 (TB) passes Lee Station on the RMs' very short-lived operation on new route 261. This had replaced the Lewisham to Bromley portion of the 94 in September 1982, but converted to LS O.P.O. in April 1983. It contrasts with a DMS following on route 75. The railway bridge here had to be slightly altered to allow these taller buses to pass beneath it.

The RTs which had for many years dominated the scene at Eltham Church are now but a memory as RM918 (SP) escorts a Titan on route 132 on 22nd June 1983. At this period, the 161 was also worked by the latter type as crew-operated buses from Plumstead Garage, where they had recently replaced MDs.

Route 190's Old Coulsdon, Tudor Rose terminus was right on the southern edge of the Central Area, yet nevertheless still within the London Borough of Croydon. On 16th August 1984, RM308 (TC) on the stand there contrasts with two London Country AN-class Leyland Atlanteans on route 409.

Short-Lived Workings

As referred to earlier in these pages, most RM operation on local routes in South East London was short-lived. On of their briefest allocations of all was that on the Sunday 124A, which gained them on 25th July 1971 but was converted to DMS O.M.O. on 9th January 1972. On 19th September 1971, RM214 (TL) reverses on the edge of Dartford Heath outside Bexley Mental Hospital before returning to Forest Hill.

Parent route 124 likewise had only just over four months of RM operation. On 11th December 1971, RM1336 (TL) heads along Dunkery Road, Mottingham on a section or route unique to the 124 and 124A just four weeks before DMS O.M.O. conversion.

Route 51A's period of RM operation was even shorter, since they progressively replaced RTs in the last two weeks of January 1977, only for the route to be withdrawn on 21st May. A week before its last day, RM486 (SP) heads past Woolwich Dockyard on one of the route's rush hour journeys to Charlton Station on 13th May 1977.

New route 261, which replaced the Lewisham to Bromley section of the 94 on 4th September 1982 and then the 47 between Bromley and Farnborough and the 51 between Farnborough and Orpington, was only RM operated until 23rd April 1983, when O.P.O. LSs replaced them. On 12th March 1983, some six weeks beforehand, RM47 (TB) passes Orpington Hospital.

Market Day

Many locations in South East London are famous for their markets and shopping centres. Bromley is typical, and on 9th December 1967, RT788 (TL) loads up at Bromley Market Place with Christmas shoppers when heading for Shoreditch on the 47. It wrongly shows a slipboard relating to route 54's diversion in Elmers End.

Dusk falls on the same short winter's afternoon as RTL238 (PR) also loads up with Christmas shoppers on route 108A, bound for the other Bromley - Bromley-By-Bow in Eltham High Street. This was the last Christmas that RTLs operated - the last of them having perished on 30th November 1968.

A little later on the same occasion, market stalls' lights illuminate Beresford Square, Woolwich as RT4001 (AM) sets off on a short working of route 99 (whose full route went to Erith) to Upper Belvedere. In the foreground are the tram tracks which had been abandoned more than fifteen years previously.

Another street market in the area is at the northern end of Lewisham High Road, where Saunders-bodied RT4398 (TB) is approaching its terminus on one of the 47's many short workings there from Farnborough on 15th July 1968.

Christmas shoppers from the nearby Deptford Market are evident as RM1041 (NX) heads for Abbey Wood on the New Cross Saturday allocation of route 177 on 11th December 1971, four weeks before this tram replacement route converted from RT to DMS O.M.O.

Bromley Market Place is thronged with shoppers as RT2893 (TB) sets off on route 119 for West Croydon on 3rd October 1972, having just emerged from the one-way system there. Of note is the bus stop on the right, where intending passengers are instructed to queue on one side from some routes, and on the other for the rest of them.

Peckham town centre is always busy, and this view of RT1868 (ED) heading to route 12's western extremity at Harlesden on 16th February 1973 typifies it in the early 1970s. Of note is the Greater London Council van on the left. This entity had replaced the former London County Council (and most of Middlesex County Council's functions together with those of County Boroughs such as East and West Ham and Croydon) in 1965, and I was employed by it at this time. The mere thought of its destruction in 1986 by the Thatcher regime was unthinkable in 1973!

A well-laden RT2514 (BX) rounds Bexleyheath Clock Tower on 18th July 1974, no doubt catering for shoppers at the nearby market. Route 229 had been extended to replace the 698 trolleybus, whose terminus this had been, via Erith, Abbey Wood and Plumstead to Woolwich, amid the first stage of the trolleybus conversion programme on 4th March 1959.

Back at Woolwich, Beresford Square, the market is in full swing on 12th October 1974 as RM21 (NX) pulls out into the High Street, where tram tracks are beginning to resurface to meet those still in situ in the square! Route 192 had converted to RM operation on Saturdays a week before, and would gain them daily in May 1976.

On 12th July 1975, RT492 (TB) collects shoppers at Lewisham Market when working route 94's Saturday extension to Brockley Rise, which supplemented route 122 over its Lee Green to Brockley Rise section.

The crowds mill around outside Allders' department store in Croydon's busy North End as RM348 (TB) heads for Bromley North on Saturday route 119A on 17th April 1976. It passes the historic almshouses on the corner of George Street. Allders store closed in 2012 after some 150 years trading.

Cobbs department store in Sydenham was one of South East London's most prestigious, giving its name to Cobbs Corner which RT1881 (AM) negotiates on is journey from Bexleyheath to Crystal Palace on 6th April 1978. Route 122 converted to RM operation just over two weeks later, whilst Cobbs ceased trading in 1981.

On 22nd April 1978, route 122's first day of RM operation, RM218 (AM) escorts RM738 (AW) out of Beresford Square, Woolwich. The street market is as busy as ever, but the tram tracks have disappeared under new road surfacing.

On 20th November 1982, both DMS2054 (BX) on route 96 and the MD following on the 180 in a busy Powis Street, Woolwich will soon be withdrawn and replaced by new Titans. Ironically, the DMS would return to South East London in 1986 for some four and a half years working for independent operator Metrobus of Orpington on L.R.T. contracts for such routes as the 61!

Borough Market is much closer to Central London, located just south of London Bridge. On 21st June 1983, RM201 (PR) heads past its main entrance into Borough High Street bound for Herne Hill on route 40, as B20 DMS2473 (WD) sets off for Mitcham on route 44. This type of DMS survived south of the Thames until the early 1990s, whilst crew Titans replaced RMs on route 40 in 1984.

Fast-forwarding in time by more than twenty years, RML2683 (Q) collects passengers in Walworth Road outside busy East Street Market on 26th October 2004. By now, routes 12 and 36 are the only crew-operated routes in South East London, and the 12 will convert to bendibus operation a week after I took this photograph. However, not only those contraptions, but also all of the low-floor double-deckers visible in this photograph are now past history too!

Illustrating the bendibuses that replaced Routemasters on route 12, MAL82 (Q) heads into Peckham town centre in June 2009, by which time these vehicles were all due to be replaced by conventional O.P.O. buses. It is in Rye Lane, where a street trader sells his wares adjacent to the Chicken Cottage, an establishment that would probably have been favoured by Joe Meek and Wilfrid Brambell!

At Home

Catford Garage is still going strong today, having its origins with the Thomas Tilling concern, which explains its code "TL" (Tilling Lewisham). On 17th December 1967, Saunders-bodied RT2900 (TL) has just run in after a stint on the Sunday 124A.

In contrast, the splendid Peckham Garage, built on the site of the bombed Bull Yard premises in connection with tram replacement was closed in 1993 and a supermarket built on its site in the centre of town - typical of the Thatcher regime's puppet L.R.T's policies. In happier times on 18th February 1968, Saunders-bodied RT2397 is out of action there, feared at the time to be the first Saunders RTs withdrawn of their last overhaul cycle, of which it was one of the first to be done in March 1965. In the event, it was moved to Merton Garage where it remained in service until January 1970. It accompanies Peckham trainer RTW487.

A little further to the east, New Cross Garage was, and still is, one of London's biggest having been rebuilt from what had been one of the last tram depots in use. On 4th May 1968, recently-overhauled RT2806 (NX) has run in on tram replacement route 182, which will be withdrawn in June. The building behind it is not part of the garage, but New Cross Synagogue, which had been destroyed during the 1940 blitz (the tram depot being damaged too) but completely rebuilt in 1956. Sadly, it closed in 1985 and has since been used as a Chinese restaurant.

A second new bus garage was built in Peckham in conjunction with tram replacement, on the site of the former London County Council tram maintenance works in Bellenden Road. It closed on 22nd March 1969: this view was taken on its final evening, with an RT and an RM about to move around the corner to Peckham Garage. The lorry in the "cubby hole" in the centre of the picture is 1014MY, a solitary Maudslay Marathon fuel tanker dating from 1944, and purchased by LT in 1947. The garage was used for many years after closure by the Post Office, but housing occupies the site today.

Bexleyheath Garage is unique amongst all London bus garages as having been built new as a trolleybus depot, in 1935. It was one of the first two such to convert to motor bus operation in March 1959. On 20th September 1969, RT2033 (BX) stands outside, representing its then all-RT allocation. Route 96 had replaced the 696 trolleybus and converted to DMS O.M.O. in 1971.

Bromley Garage on the Hastings Road south of Bromley Common, also still with us today, is another former Tilling establishment, hence its code TB ("Tilling Bromley"). It is often used as a terminus for other garage's buses, as is so on 1st September 1972, as RT4356 (TL) departs on route 47 for Shoreditch. One of the SMSs based there for the 227 is also visible. In more recent times, an additional yard for the garage has been provided on the left hand side of the road facing the camera.

On 26th February 1975, a somewhat battered RT3892 (SP) sets off for Woolwich on route 161 from Sidcup Garage. This former London General Omnibus Company garage, despite being modernised in 1977, was closed in 1986, largely owing to loss of work by routes being tendered out to other operators.

On the same day as the previous picture, RT4195 (NX) is a spreadover bus that has run in to New Cross Garage after the morning rush hour, subbing for an RM. New Cross' still large allocation of RTs was being decimated at this time, with route 1 having been converted to RM operation a month previously, and route 21 about to convert two days later. The last RTs there (from route 192) departed on 1st May 1976.

For most of the 1950s up until the summer of 1966, Camberwell Garage had an all-RTL allocation, following which RTs replaced them and also RMs became allocated for such routes as the 35, 40/A and 159. By 31st July 1975 when RT441 and RT549 (Q) stand facing Warner Road, their small allocation on route 172 was all that was left, and that converted to crew DM a month later. A couple of rogue RTs were allocated briefly two years after that. Camberwell Garage is still going strong today.

On 14th May 1977, RT2879 (BX) lays over outside Bexleyheath Garage when working route 89, whilst a Plumstead RT which has terminated there on the 122 keeps it company. The 89 would be this garage's last RT route in April 1978. In its original incarnation as a trolleybus depot, Bexleyheath was unlucky enough to receive direct hits both in the 1940 blitz and from flying bombs later in the war.

RT3771 (AM) departs from the old Plumstead Garage for Crystal Palace on 21st April 1978, route 122's last day of RT operation. This former London General garage on the corner of Wickham Lane and Kings Highway was closed at the end of October 1981 and replaced by the new Plumstead Garage opposite Plumstead Station.

Another old London General garage to close in 1981 was the one at Norwood. On its final day, 25th April 1981, RM2071, RM818 and RM2038 stand in the garage entrance. In this case, the garage was demolished and completely rebuilt on the same site, also being enlarged and occupying adjacent land hitherto used for housing. It reopened in 1984 and is still in use today.

Abbey Wood was originally a London County Council tram depot, and should have been converted for trolleybus operation but for the war. In common with New Cross, it operated London's last trams in July 1952, then became a bus garage. In its last year or so it was entirely stocked with MD-class Metro-Scania Metropolitans, of which MD118 and MD125 (AW) stand outside on 18th October 1981, a couple of weeks before it too was closed and replaced by the new Plumstead Garage.

Somewhat bizarrely, RT2958 - by now one of the last RTs still in London Transport stock - stands outside the new Plumstead Garage on 30th October 1981, the day before it opened. Used as a mobile unit to train crews on the use of radio route control, it has been used to bring publicity to the area for posting on bus stops and so on advising on route changes resulting from the new garage's opening.

Walworth Garage was another built as a result of tram replacement, on the site of the old Camberwell L.C.C. tram depot opposite Camberwell Garage in Camberwell New Road. On 3rd September 1982, DMS1911 (TL) has terminated there on route 185, on which it sets off for Blackwall Tunnel, Delta Metal Works in the company of two RMs. The garage was closed in November 1985, again a victim of L.R.T. route tendering, but fortunately survived to reopen subsequently, and is still in use today.

    South East London

By 11th September 1983, Catford Garage had been enlarged to include an open parking area outside a former filling station and car showroom next door to it. B20 DMSs 2447, 2448 and 2490 stand outside it. All were replaced by new Titans shortly after this picture was taken, but were transferred to such garages as Merton and Sutton, where they lasted into the early 1990s. The buildings behind them were later demolished, thus enlarging the space for bus parking.

Elmers End Garage was severely damaged when it received a direct hit from a flying bomb in 1944, resulting in virtually complete rebuilding in the early 1950s. On 18th October 1986, RM635 (ED) sets off to take up service on route 12 at Norwood Junction, flanked by an LS and a DMS a week before this splendid garage's closure.

On the same day as the previous picture, DMS2461 (ED) is one of two of this unfortunate class running in to Elmers End Garage on route 194, as another changes crew. Much outrage was caused to passengers and staff alike by this garage's closure, and this has neither been forgotten nor forgiven thirty-three years later!

South Croydon Garage is situated on the Brighton Road, about half way between Croydon town centre and Purley. It was originally a Thomas Tilling Garage, opened in 1916. In addition to the main entrance/exit flanking the main road, it also has entrances at each side. On 30th August 1972, RT4671 has recently been withdrawn after running in from route 197 and stands just inside the Crunden Road entrance on the north side of the garage. One of the XAs used on routes 233, 234/B and C1-C4 stands behind it.

Displayed outside South Croydon Garage's main entrance, D2629 (TC) is adorned in an approximation of Croydon Tramways' chocolate and grey livery to mark London Transport's Golden Jubilee, for which an open day was held at the garage on 7th May 1983. Sadly, the garage received a direct hit during the Blitz in 1941, and had to be completely rebuilt after the war. As a result it has a "mini-Aldenham" maintenance section at the rear, which still sees much use with the garage's present operator, Arriva London.

Rural Rides

Many bus routes on the outer edge of South East London pass through some splendid rural scenery. Route 146 is a good example, on which RT1100 (TB) head along Baston Road through Hayes Common on one of the route's short workings to Keston, Fox on 1st September 1972.

Chislehurst Common, with the famous caves nearby, is another pleasant rural setting. On 18th September 1973, RT2892 (SP) has just set off for Eltham, Well Hall Station when passing through it. Route 228 no longer exists in this area today, having been withdrawn in November 1986.

Yet another common in the area is Farnborough Common, through which RT3655 (TL) approaches route 47's southern terminus on 23rd September 1973. Route 47 was cut back from its long-standing terminus here to Bromley Garage in September 1982, and replaced by new route 261.

Some pleasant rural scenery exists between Bexleyheath and Sidcup in Bridgen, where RM532 (SP) is captured on film, also heading for Farnborough, on 27th September 1977. The route was extended there upon conversion from RT to RM operation in May 1977, replacing the 51, but cut back again to Orpington and also converted to O.P.O. in September 1982, also replaced by new route 261 through Farnborough.

The outermost section of route 146, between Keston and Downe, is more rural still. On 29th October 1977, RT3778 (TB) heads along New Road Hill approaching route 146's southern terminus at Downe. It is hard to believe that this section of route is within Greater London!

It is not often that RMs on Central Area routes encountered horse riders, but on 2nd January 1981, RM51 (AW) does so at route 161's Chislehurst War Memorial terminus, in the middle of the common. Is that Isle riding her white horse?

Just under three months before its cut-back again to Orpington, and conversion to O.P.O. a somewhat bedraggled RM843 (SP) passes through Farnborough Common at the southern end of route 229.

On route 47's replacement between Bromley Garage and Farnborough, RM47 (TB) also heads through Farnborough Common on 12th March 1983. The route continued through Farnborough, rather than terminating there, to also replace the 229 as far as Orpington, overlapping it along the High Street. LS O.P.O. single-deckers replaced the RMs six weeks after this picture was taken.

Looking like a rural scene, RM2012 (PM) in fact escorts one of its fellows on route 63 past leafy Peckham Rye Common on 4th September 1985. At this time, Peckham was often looked upon as a "third world" slum, but has since become "yuppified" apparently.

Buses In Trouble

In their later years, RTs had a tendency to overheat, especially when well-laden and climbing hills. RT192 (AW), then the lowest-numbered RT in service, has done so when calling at Eltham Church on 30th April 1977, having climbed up from Well Hall Station on route 161A. It was withdrawn and sold for scrap in June.

Also badly overheating, RT1791 (BX) has turned short at Welling, Springfield Road and for some reason has a blank via blind on 19th April 1978, three days before route 89 converted to DMS O.P.O. However, it survived to be transferred to Barking Garage for another six months' service.

The sight of a Routemaster broken down at the roadside was very rare, right up until the time they were finally withdrawn in 2005. However, RM1331 (TB) has let the side down in Orpington on 21st April 1983, the penultimate day of the 261's short-lived RM operation.